Everyday
Life in
Two Worlds

A Psychic's Experience

Everyday Life in Two Worlds

A Psychic's Experience

Kelly Joyce Neff

HAMPTON ROADS
PUBLISHING COMPANY, INC.

Cover photo by Kathleen Rhodes
Cover design by Patrick Smith

For information write:

Hampton Roads Publishing Company, Inc.
891 Norfolk Square
Norfolk, VA 23502

Or call: (804)459-2453
FAX: (804)455-8907

If you are unable to order this book from your local
bookseller, you may order directly from the publisher.
Quantity discounts for organizations are available.
Call 1-800-766-8009, toll-free.

ISBN 1-878901-95-8

Printed on acid-free paper
in the United States of America

Dedicated to Irene and the Gang
For their constant and sometimes unwanted support
Hey guys, save me a Newcastle and some green M&Ms!

A hundred and eight thanks to:

Danny Lliteras, *for acting on a dream, without which
this book would not have been written.*

Frank DeMarco and Bob Friedman, *for having faith in me,
without which this never would have seen the light
of day. Thanks too for the facilitation
of all things Virginian!*

Wendy Dodd, *for keeping the faith, and bringing me
into the Eternal Circle this time around.*

Cathleen, *my old one, for Always Being There. Om.*

Kevin, *for letting it be. Peace be with you.*

Contents

Introduction

"Everyday Life in Two Worlds" may sound like a New Age soap opera, but I assure you that such an assumption is. . .entirely correct! At least sometimes; when the moon is in one's natal sign, and all the heavy *sturm und drang* planets are in conjunction, which they currently are at this writing. The astral and physical plane antics resulting from this resemble something between any column of Erma Bombeck's and any episode of "Father Knows Best." That is to say, What is Real?

What is real? Ay, there's the rub! As quoth the Melancholy Dane, "There are more things in heaven and earth, Horatio, than are dreamt of in your philosophy," and the world is, at long last in my considered opinion, coming to know it. Speaking as one who has spent the last thirty-odd years (give or take a couple of millennia) on the far end of weird, I welcome the chance for once to appear relatively normal and mainstream.

I have been called "organically weird" by a witty and affectionate friend, and what began as a joke contains the seeds of wisdom, as truth is so oft spoke in jest. The phrase has become a tag for people like me and is used with some frequency in this book. However humourous and off-centre it might be, it is not lightly applied but deadly accurate, as a peek in Noah Webster will adduce:

ORGANIC: *adj.* Latin from the Greek—*oganikos;* 5: forming an integral element of a whole. Fundamental, vital, inherent; constitutionally. . .

WEIRD: *adv.* Middle, Old English—*wird, wyrd*—from Old Norse—*urthr* (weird, fate). Related to Old English *wearthan* (to become); 1: fate, destiny, lot, fortune; 2: (Scottish) to foretell or ascertain as a fate; 3: (archaic) 1): of or relating to, or dealing with Fate or the Fates; 2) (a): of or relating to witchcraft or the supernatural; (b): unearthly, mysterious.

For it has come to my attention with increasing frequency that many people who are coming to terms—as I have done—with the fact that they *have never been* "normal," but are only just now realizing it; that they perchance find this sudden insight of "abnormality" painful and that they are seeking to understand how they "got" this way, and is there anybody else out there of the same experience.

Rest assured, gentle reader, there are and have been, despite every mainstream evidence to the contrary. Like Holmes, you simply have to know how to look at things in the proper way and it's all perfectly clear. Elementary. . .and it doesn't require a seven-percent solution or other mind-altering substances to figure it out.

Having been a sojourner on this path a goodly while, and learnt the ways of the Mohicans, Delaware, and sundry locals, I feel it behooves me to share with you, fellow wanderer, some of my observations. Such is the purpose of this book, not merely to spin a tale across an evening's camp-fire, but to leave a map of where I have been for those who come after. May it be of aid and comfort to you. May it provoke you into states of joy and peace. May it be just what you needed. May it ease your mind according to your bearings, and speed you on your journey. Each one of you reading this, though I never meet you, has my love.

Namaste.

Kelly Joyce Neff
Williamsburg, Virginia
May, 1994.

Chapter One

ॐ

Through the Looking Glass; or, I am Born.

Studying the manner of one's birth often leads to the most pertinent insights into oneself and the path one is on. This is perhaps contemplating one's navel to an umpth degree, but it is nonetheless useful. If the obvious maternal connection is lacking due to one's own age there are always family stories to rely on ("You know, Joe just *had* to come in the middle of a tornado on Hallowe'en. . ."); or, failing that, rebirthing or regression.

However the information comes back, the organically weird will often find that, from their first appearance, their lives were marked as being different. There being no gratuitous scenes in this little play we are enacting called Planet Earth, paying attention to the stage directions ought to be the first task of the player.

In my own case, my twin sister and I were quite a surprise to our parents, a pair of unmarried college students, especially as we came three months early, one Sunday afternoon, which just happened to be St. Patrick's Day, when Mum and her roommates were planning to go to a party. The party was definitely over when Joyce and Marie came home to find my mother in a puddle. Four hours later, at sunset, we made our appearance. Folklorists take note: sunset is one of the magical times of day, as are sunrise, noon, and midnight, when the gateway to the Otherworld is open, and anything may—and often does—happen.

The plot thickened when Patricia and Kelly turned out to be two redheads. In most of the world's mythologies, twins are regarded with awe or suspicion (sometimes both), a blessing or a curse from the gods. In Celtic mythology, which is my primary focus, every hero or heroine comes in twos or threes, which represent either the dark/light aspect of the soul (twins), or the three levels of being: physical, mental, and spiritual (triplets). And redheads are traditionally Otherworldly beings, members of the faery race, and are likewise regarded with respect and suspicion. So there was Patty, the dark redhead, firstborn, and Kelly, the fair redhead, second born. Celtic mythology personified.

My mother probably wondered at, and regretted, her letter to her brother two years before (long before she met our father), wherein she wrote, "Ha ha, tell Ma I'm in the hospital and just gave birth to twin girls. . ." My grandmother, from whom I had this story and my mother's letters—for she had been long since dead by this time—recognized a fatedness to my mother's words, with a sorrowful hindsight, for she had not been aware of us at the time of our coming into being.

My sister decided she didn't care for this scene at all and beat a hasty retreat, four days after our birth, leaving yours truly as the smallest baby ever to survive at UCLA hospital. I weighed 740 grams, or about a pound and ten ounces, or two apples and an orange. This sort of struggle for life at an early age is rife in the mythologies of heroes (or heroines). It is almost *de rigueur*.

My hero-tale is no different. In the first six months, I had several periods of apnea (lack of breath) from which I had to be resuscitated, an unexplained head enlargement, rubella, and scarlet fever. I was almost lost several times. They didn't know if I would develop normally, or be blind, or deaf, or retarded. (I remembered this with a smirk when I was on the Dean's List for several years running in college. Retarded indeed!) But it was my first trial. Like a hopeful would-be Buddhist monk sitting outside the lamasery for days on end, meditating, I proved my worth for the course before me.

The odds for survival had definitely been in my sister's favour, for she weighed two pounds and three ounces at birth, yet she reneged and went back home again, leaving me to fight on alone. I wondered at the reason for this until I did a birth regression, and the answer came ringing clear.

Mea Culpa. I admit it, I kicked her out ahead of me because I wanted to be born on St. Patrick's day. I had things to do, people to see. I didn't want to be a Gemini.

So began the little miracle.

When you ask people about their earliest memory, the age to which they have recall is often as illuminating as the incident itself. Kevin, my former husband, remembers the night before his fourth birthday; my grandfather cannot remember his mother being a redhead—for hair turns white early in our family—though she was twenty-four when he was born. His earliest memory is at about age seven. It seems to me that there is a correlation between memory and the manifestation of what is now called psychic phenomenon. I mean to say that those who manifest such often have flashes of memory at remarkably early ages. As we know from *The Miracle Worker*, Helen Keller remembered an incident when she was eighteen months old. My own first memory is earlier than that, and I thought nothing of it until I began to tell people about it. Then I realized how uncanny it was, for it was met with either astonishment or disbelief. Until that time, I thought everyone could remember very early incidents of their lives.

Everyone remembers where they were when Jack Kennedy was shot, but in my case I was an infant being held over the shoulder by my foster mother, and I watched the news footage on the television from that vantage point. She was hushing her children, saying "This is important." Then there was John John waving, saluting, at the funeral. And the thought, "Wait a minute! This wasn't supposed to happen. . ." There was the definite knowing that Kennedy's death was not the major pathway chosen in his life, but a detour due to something having gone wrong earlier. This knowing came in a flash, full-blown, as most telepathic knowing and messages from beyond. If asked to explain how you know it, you can't. You "just know it" on a visceral level.

This *knowing* goes beyond the age-appropriate understanding of the person, child or adult, which is why children often say some of the remarkable things they do, which most adults tend to ignore as fantasy or blow off because they're too weird to deal with. Junior can't possibly have said X; he's only two years old. But to look at it in a more balanced way: Junior is a fully integrated being currently inhabiting a two-year-old body, and sometimes the integration leaks out around the two-year-oldness and he says inexplicable things. And the farther along that integrated being is on his or her path, the more frequently these leaks will happen. In some cases, it's more leak than two-year-old.

I have seen this with my own children. My oldest son, when he began to talk in sentences, had a pronounced New York accent, when neither my husband nor I, nor anyone with whom Rudraigh was in contact, had ever been to New York. He also had a thing about trains. In a book shop in Dublin, when I was doing fieldwork for my thesis, he sat on the floor enraptured by a coffee-table-sized book, *The Encyclopaedia of Trains*. He was, I point out, two years old. Well, the book cost £75, and we persuaded him (through a disappointed tantrum) to pick another one. He chose *The Belfast and County Down Railway,* which was a very serious history of that route and its trains and schedules. He would examine—"read"—the timetables for hours. Upon enquiry to my guides when we arrived back in San Francisco, I discovered that Rudraigh had been a train conductor in New York in the late 1930s and early '40s. So, he happily read the timetables, and slept with the book for two years. Positively refused to go to bed without it, as some children do with their teddy bears.

For my own part, the shooting of JFK is not my only early memory. I recall too my foster-mother's face, the configuration of the house (confined to the stairs, the hall, the kitchen, and the living room), and—vaguely—her own two young children. These are flashes, like snapshots in an album, bringing with them all kinds of sensory memories.

One of my college lecturers, a Breton/Turkish/Irish woman by the name of Laurie Fadave, had a memory even earlier. She described to her mother a visit to a very old lady when she was a baby, described the lady and very specific details of the room. Her mother turned white and said, "You can't remember that! That was the day we brought you home from the hospital!" But the visit had never been talked about—it was merely a courtesy call, and not one to an esteemed relation—and the lady they visited died shortly afterward, so there was no doubt of the authenticity of Laurie's memory.

When I was older (all of a year and a half) I was sitting on the floor, looking up at a visitor of my mother's, and found myself thinking how frightened she was inside her very-together exterior; I saw the state of her soul, as clearly exposed as the emperor and his new suit of clothes. And I wondered: how could she live so long and still be uncomfortable in her own skin? I think I made her nervous, looking at her. She wondered if I knew her secret, and thought herself crazy for wondering. This was a baby, wasn't it?

I never thought so. Nor did I think of myself as child. That creature down there walking along the dusty road singing a song with the faeries was a child, but I was not. The solitary creature observing the play of others from a remove was a young and growing child, but I had no age. I simply was. When in this little play I played the role of a child, I believed everyone thought this way, for everyone in my Otherworld shared my perceptions of reality; all the animals, my faery friends, and plant devas.

I found the physical world absolutely fascinating, never having been where I happened to live then: southern California. My last life experience had been as a beatnik cocaine addict in Liverpool after the Second World War. Quite a different experience, which came fully clear in my consciousness only this year [1994]. Before that, there were strong resonances, but I thought them aberrations. By comparison, the suburbs of Los Angeles, land of sunshine and oranges, was a vacation to an exotic foreign country. I was in love with life, exploring everything. This is the blessing of an unrestricted childhood, the birthright of all children, to live in the natural, magical state of Wonderland as long as they can (though some of us never have left).

I would spend long periods of time examining myself in every regard, the body's construction, its peculiarities. Part of this was not having been a female in a while, but a good deal of it was due to still spending large amounts of time in the ethers with an astral body. What was this miracle of material existence? How did it come to be so solid when my Otherworldly friends could walk through objects? And why could this little body not fly as I did when I was apart from it? What was it made of? I was a Buddhist, seeking to understand the nature of reality through enquiry, without the words for it.

I bear many scars from many a childhood "accident," and these were the results of testing the capabilities of this thing I cart my soul about in, and making some attempt to understand its uniqueness. I was fascinated by anatomy and physiology. However, my parents would probably have appreciated it better if I'd simply asked for a copy of *Gray's Anatomy* for Christmas, instead of making constant trips to the hospital emergency room.

For instance, when I was seven I went to a birthday party at my next-door neighbour's house. Afterwards, she and her brothers and I were playing tag on their enclosed porch. I, with one of the boys chasing after me, made to run outdoors. Unfortunately, I put my left knee through their sliding glass door, as I had thought it was open.

All time stopped. I don't think anyone on the porch was breathing except me. I really had no cognizance of what had happened. I felt no pain, did not notice the shattered glass before me. I was absorbed in the sight of my knee under my fingers, with the dark blood oozing out and running down my leg. I thought to myself, watching that little girl that was me from far away, "I wonder what it looks like?" So I opened my hands slowly, as if opening a prayer book in church. It was a mass of blood and torn flesh, tendons, and white bone. One of the boys—Joey—came up beside me on the right.

"Are you all right?" he asked. He was Filipino, but even so, he looked a little pale. I looked at him, and all the sensory stimuli came rushing. Pain hit my knee like lightning, and I screamed. I kept on screaming until their mother came rushing out.

I was carried home, and the next thing I knew I was in the ER with a very nervous intern, who was trying to stitch my leg. The room smelled of ether and betadine. I was painted yellow with the stuff. I wanted to see what he was doing to my leg, and complained that he hurt me, as he hadn't waited for the anaesthetic to take effect, or else I have a high tolerance for it, which is entirely possible. In any case, he did a poor job of suturing, with which I am unsatisfied to this day. I say as a midwife now, as I did as a physician in Egypt, "I can do better than that!"

When I was eight, we were out camping in the mountains near Bakersfield, and I and my playmates were atop a high rock. The older girl who was with us—Rita was her name—told me to look out for black widow spiders, "'cause they're poisonous." Well, I took one look at a probably harmless spider and decided the ground was safer. I thought nothing of leaping the ten or twelve feet to the ground. I floated down from such heights with the astral body all the time. So I jumped. For my pains, I blacked out, cut open my chin, mangled my tongue, and knocked loose a few teeth. I ate soup for weeks and bore my mother's shaking head every time she looked at me.

Whenever I went to the doctor, I was never bored with the long wait. I was forever poking into jars and tins and cupboards, looking to see what had changed in the pharmacopoeia and instruments. And there was always a sense of this, "looking to see what had changed." For I have practiced medicine many times, in one way or another. I never felt so at home as amid the mummies and the surgical equipment at the Rosicrucian Museum in San Jose, California. I rubbed my hands in delight at the scalpels and studied with a critical eye the manner of wrapping mummies and mummified body parts; and gave forth to one *tourista* on the manner of extracting and preserving brains from the bodies. When she remarked that I plainly knew something of Egyptian medicine, I just smiled.

So I slowly learned the generally accepted limitations of the physical body, but not of the world. Often and often I would sit and wonder, if I held out my hand and touched that tree or that window or whatever, would it really be there? Was it all an illusion, something I had made up in my own mind? Would my hand go through it?

My faery friends were about me, playful sometimes, earnest at other times, always just a slight unfocus of the eyes, a slight tuning of the ears away. It was not a question of belief, for no one had ever told me of them. Now, there are many earnest and well-intentioned people (mostly folklorists, whose jobs depend on it) who say that to exist at all, faeries require a belief in them. This is nonsense. I neither believed nor disbelieved in them, and yet they were always about me. I was, in their words, "one of them." They are everywhere in the world, in every country, in every time.

What are they, that which I call faeries? Despite my admittedly Celtic bent—and even though the word for them is generally accepted as Celtic—they are in no way restricted to leprechauns (of the Lucky Charms or Disney variety or otherwise) or the British Isles.

They are, most simply, the elemental spirits of a place. They have a slightly different vibrational frequency from "regular" folks (human beings, that is), which is why most people can't see them (much as human beings cannot hear dog whistles but a dog can, or see the wind, but pigs can. . .so they say). But their existence is as "real" to them as ours is to us, and it's mighty impolite of some people to say they do not exist.

If you live in a cardboard box and know only the reality of the interior of the cardboard box and deny the possibility of there being something outside your box, then you are ever doomed to your dull little reality, which may be fine for you; but it doesn't give you the right to confine someone else to it. That's coercion. Karma. Bad News.

As any tweedy folklorist can tell you, there are four types of faeries—earth, air, fire, and water—with various subcategories, depending on the terrain in which you live. This is where Walt Disney and his depictions come in. He was very fond of the earth and water varieties, though the air faeries had their pin-up girl in Tinkerbell. Faeries are the spirit or soul of the place they inhabit, the personification of the landscape, the reason we can speak of the natural world in any way other than scientific. When the poets speak of the beauties of nature, it is the faeries who are their muses.

One of my most memorable experiences with the fey folk happened not in childhood, but when I was doing fieldwork in Ireland. That whole adventure was full of encounters with Them, but one I recall particularly occurred when we had stopped at the neolithic passage grave at Knowth, in County Meath.

Knowth, Dowth, and Newgrange—or Brugh naBoinne—form a triad of power points, linked by that subtle and mysterious force known as ley lines, and connect with other such sites in Ireland,

England, and Europe. Knowth when I visited it was in the years-long process of excavation (archaeology being glorified grave-robbing or digging in dead people's garbage for a living), and was covered over in green plastic that bore a suspicious resemblance to large garbage bags.

It was a soft day, as the Irish say—meaning it was dreary because it had rained and was about to rain again—with the sky all a brooding mass of teakettle-steam clouds, and as I stood upon the makeshift parapet, separated from the site by an equally makeshift cyclone fence, I heard the distinct sound of faery music, with its eerie, high, sweet tones, quite indescribable. Then, as if becoming aware of my presence, the music ceased, and there emerged from the green plastic shroud a multitude of the faery host with their tall slim bodies, wraith-like, moving out onto the mound of rubble beside their destroyed home.

They were of a pale blue-white colour, sharp of feature and sonorous of voice. One of them, a young man, betook himself to be their spokesman and addressed me while the rest carried on, wailing and lamenting, in funereal fashion behind him.

"See what they have done," he said, gesturing toward the grave mound. "See what they have done to our home. We are put out into the rain like tinkers walking the roads. You are one of us. You must do something. You must do something to restore our home to us!"

I was overcome. My heart was thudding in my aching throat, and tears fell like rain down my cheeks.

"I can do nothing!" I told him in grief. "I am but one woman against the lot of scientists. They would seek to understand, but they do not know what is beneath their very noses. But they will not listen to me; they have never listened to me. I'm sorry!"

This faery fellow took on an horrific aspect as he moved himself suddenly within inches of me. The wind came up, howling, and the rain began pelting down, only on me, as I discovered later. He was Crom Dubh, the Crooked Black One personified, and I shrank back from him.

"You will do something!" He insisted. "You are one of us. You owe it to us—"

Trembling, I swore I would, and he returned to his comely former self. The wind dropped, the rain ceased, and he made me a handsome, courtly bow. "Until we meet again," he said, and disappeared with the rest of the *sidhe* back into the faery mound. The glittering air was then dull again and I was left standing alone on the parapet.

Such tactics may strike some as coercion, but they had their effect.

I went down directly and wrote out a poem called *The Green Shroud*, which I distributed amongst my anthropology friends back home. I certainly have never viewed archaeology in the same way since!

As a child, my experiences of Them were peaceful, and as natural as breathing. They were my little friends, under every leaf and flower. There were brown, apple-wizened little people in autumn; grey-white-haired Old Ones in winter; tender, childlike playmates in spring; and voluptuous hedonists in ripe summer. When faced in college with the "information" that eddies of leaves moving along the land in the wind was the faery troop passing by; or that dust motes contained dancing faeries; or that a certain ear crimp (which I and my children have) was a mark of feyness; or that impetigo and other less savoury forms of "creeping crud" were "faery blight," my response was "but of course!" for I had seen them so my whole life (and have always had recurring bouts of impetigo, as do my children). I have always heard faery music and thought, until I went to school, that everyone else did too.

The current trend in children's toys for iridescence in pastel colours, or holographic, swirling rainbow brilliance is simply the world opening up to this other reality, for that is how the world truly is. When you see the emanations of an object, its aura, its true essence, this is how it is viewed. As an adult, I am yet very conscious of the magical world in which children live, the truth of the colours they are allowed to play with; the resonance of the tinkling music they are offered with toy pianos, music boxes, wind-up lullaby animals, and such. The latter is pure faery music and is why the harp is so popular in Celtic traditions. There's many the aged blind harper in "the old days" who professed to have gained his knowledge from the faeries, and having heard both species of music, fey and fey-inspired, I am not inclined to scoff!

I have always been extraordinarily lucky with the faeries wherever I have lived. They rarely have played the tricks on me of which folktales are full, perhaps because I know them a little too well. The antics they have got up to—absconding with pieces of enticing jewelry (amber has been a favourite), fouling up machinery (whether my computer or my blender, it matters not), hiding my or my children's shoes (to turn them up later in the most unlikely places)—have been largely harmless. No trees have fallen on my house, as happened to my college lecturer, Laurie Fadave, nor has my family been struck overmuch with various forms of faery blight.

Admittedly, I have long followed the old festivals and made obeisance to Their presence, not out of a sense of obligation or fear, but of connection to the land. For in the quarterly festivals, and the offset equinoxes and solstices, we have not only the cycle of the year, but the whole cycle of Life; not merely of our present mortal existence, but of our Whole Life, stretching back past comprehensible "time" into the mists of forgetting, and reaching forward into the unimaginable vistas of the Realised future. In recognising and celebrating the changes of the earth, the shifting face of the land, we are in the most profound way acknowledging the interconnectedness of all things, a concept which our Paleolithic forebears (or former selves) would have understood innately. In general, I hate cities, for therein it is very difficult to hear and feel the Mother speaking, and I believe that this disconnectedness from All That Is is *the* true cause of the world's present woes.

(Nevertheless, my "unseen" friends are kind to me, even in cities. One of the mundane benefits of this acknowledgement of Their presence is good parking karma: I can always get a space in front of where I want to be, usually with time on the meter. It helps to have friends!)

Related to the faeries are the devas. According to esoteric wisdom, they are of a lower vibration or evolution than the faeries, for they are the life energy of the plant, while the faeries are its guardians. One can spend a lifetime and never have a perfect knack with these powerful creatures. As Thomas Jefferson said of himself at seventy-three, "I am an old man, but a young gardener."

Like Tom, I too am still learning from the devas and, I suspect, always will. I have had my failures, as every gardener does (mostly when I follow the directions on the seed packages!) and I tend to have better success with outdoor plants than houseplants (once having killed a cactus—a nearly impossible feat!) which leads me to the conclusion that plants were never meant to be indoors.

This may sound like sour grapes, for we all know people with marvellous green thumbs who can grow killer tomatoes in their cat's litter box, and other wonders, but for my part, there is really nothing in container gardening to compare to getting out in all weathers and digging amongst the sweet williams or squashes.

The plant (or its deva) will tell you what it needs, if you put yourself into a meditative space. Unfocus your eyes into the middle distance, unplug your mind from the constant internal yammering, tune into the plantness of whatever you are working with, and the "voice" will be heard loud and clear. In this way I have grown potatoes and other kitchen vegetables in soil that was basically plain sand. The voice is quiet and still, easily drowned out by the noise of passing motor traffic or the internal skeptic saying "You're barmy.

This is not real." But if you follow the advice, however bizarre it may seem according to gardening books, it generally works. It can be as simple as transplanting to a sunnier location, or weeding a little thinner. The voice of wild plants differs little, save in intensity, from the voice of God (or whatever you choose to call All That Is) and, on a real level, they are the same, for the same Force animates us all.

In culling wild plants from the public areas around my neighbour-hood, or when traveling, I am generally guided to notice a particular plant, either because it is a variety I have read of but never seen or because I have some immediate practical need of it. I will be walking along, like Pooh Bear lost in a daydream, and suddenly I will look down and Bingo! There is a plant of Clary Sage, or whatever I had recently been put in mind of. Assessment of its state of health (it is never wise to gather plants directly adjacent to roadsides with heavy car traffic, for instance) will lead to a quiet (mostly internal) honour-ing of the plant's essential being and a respectful request to gather some of the parts. Sometimes permission is denied, but always for good reason. (In one case, when I was in County Clare, I was denied permission by the plant's deva to gather elder berries because it was the only surviving plant within a two-mile radius.) It is not Good Work to take parts of plants without asking (remember the apple tree's reprimand to Dorothy in *The Wizard of Oz:* "How would you like it if someone came up and picked something off of you?") or to take them when permission is denied. Both are sheer rapine, and part of the sickness that grips our planet at the moment. Don't be greedy or fearful and contribute to the difficulty! There are plenty of other plants around, willing to give of themselves if their consciousness is acknowledged. Avail instead of them.

Houseplants, by contrast, are the comatose on life support: all tubes and wires and intravenous feeding. Yes, there's brain activity, but is that really living? I have yet to meet a houseplant who wasn't stunned or sluggish when I spoke to it. "Are you talking to *me?*" (or, alternately, "Hoozat?")

Many things can be learned from plants in a reasonably native state; they yield their secrets as easily as a bride to those who are sympathetic.

When I was a very small child—under the age of three—I played "hospital" with a neighbour child, and there was a succulent plant in the yard which we sliced open to put the oozing juice on our entirely fabricated wounds. In 1994, the use of aloe to heal wounds is television commercial fare, but in suburbia in 1965 this was far-out, something only crazy old prospectors talked about, like spitting tobacco juice on snakebites.

How did I know what to do? I did what human beings have done for millions of years: I listened, and the plants told me their properties. To this day, as an herbalist I follow this practice, but I was never taught it; the plants taught me, because I listened.

In my practice as an holistic healer I never will give the same answer to two people for the same condition, or even to the same person at different times, for the subtle vibrations of the plant tell me each time what is needed.

Sometimes it works too well! Once, oatstraw and horsetail grass were recommended for a friend with shingles and a rheumatoid condition (he also happened to have high blood pressure). Well, the combination not only cleared up the shingles and the rheumatic pains, but brought his blood pressure so low he could hardly get out of bed in the morning! I had made the tincture myself, so I had no one to blame but my devas for doing their work too well. My friend lowered his intake of the herbs and all is since fine. But it points out the power of these so-called unseen forces.

[For those of you interested in the process of holistic tincturing, once the plant material is gathered in the above-described manner, clean jars are chosen, washed, and maybe blessed with a rinsing of spring water, and the plant material sorted according to size (for, if you've done your work properly in the gathering, there will be virtually nothing "unusable" in your stash), all the while asking the blessing of the plant for its essence to be distilled by alcohol. (You are warning it, basically, of what is to come.) Meditate on the individual the tincture is for, and their ailment. Ask the plant the right proportions of herb, alcohol, and water to use. See the individual getting well.

[As you begin to lay in the plant material, charge the mixture with healing energy, whether by colour vibrations, sound, reike, or whatever feels right. It helps the magical and healing process to lay a circle sprig on top of the plant material, if possible, before pouring on the alcohol, for in the circle is life without end, completeness. When the spirits are poured on, cap the jar and set it in a cool dark place to steep. The general advice about steeping is six to eight weeks' time, but I have found that tinctures tell me differing times depending on the age of the plant matter used and so on. Shaking the jar every day, swirling the mixture around, "feeling" how it is doing, listening to the plant essence, will tell you when the tincture is ready far better than some arbitrary standard.

[This method I have used with great success. It makes the whole process healing on very deep levels, both for the recipient and the practitioner. At the very least, it is a pure meditative state, both grounding and uplifting. For me, it also resonates through several hundred thousand milennia as a healer. It feels "right," and in so doing, I connect with every single one of my experiences as a healer. Therefore, the recipient has the benefit not only of my current knowledge, but of everything past and future.]

At the famous Findhorn Community on the northern coast of Scotland, initial communication with the devas took a rather more dramatic form than my simple lifelong conversation: their secretary was most astonished one day to find herself addressed by a sweet pea in the following manner:

> "I can speak to you, human. I am entirely directed by my work, which is set out and molded and which I merely bring to fruition. You have come to my awareness. My work is clear before me; the force fields are there to be brought into manifestation regardless of obstacles, and there are many obstacles on this manifested world. You think that slugs, for example, are a greater menace to me than man, but this is not so; slugs are part of the order of things, and the vegetable kingdom holds no grudge against those it feeds. But man takes what he can as a matter of course, giving no thanks, which makes us strangely hostile. Humans generally seem to know not where they are going or why. If they did, what a powerhouse they would be. If they were on the straight course of what is to be done, we could co-operate with them. I have put across my meaning and bid you farewell."

—The Magic of Findhorn

Such communications clearly point out what mystics and other supranormal types have known since time immemorial, and what the bulk of mankind has forgotten since he lived on the plains of Africa and hunted and gathered for a living: everything is alive, everything is speaking always, and we are but a fragment of the whole and should be mindful of the great power we possess and its potential abuse. We are truly one with all living things, animal, vegetable, mineral or Other.

Regarding animals, there is much nonsense going on these days in middle America about pet cemeteries, pet hotels, and pet therapists—Jungian psychology for Fifi or psionic waves for Dick the mynah bird's eating disorder, but this is not entirely ridiculous; only, as with most things, a trifle overboard in trying to balance a former imbalance. The idea is good but it is coming from the intellectual axis, and not the heart or spirit; these people are thinking about how to solve matters, rather than letting the matter tell them how it wants to be solved. All that is required is being quiet and listening. You may or may not believe what you hear, or *that* you hear, or where it comes from, but that is almost immaterial.

When I was very young, I used to sit in the yard under the elm trees and talk to the birds. Not aloud, but telepathically, and when I asked, they would come down near me and answer questions of mine. It was a small thing, but consistent, and has remained so throughout my life.

In folk traditions, birds are the messengers of the Otherworld, and various birds have their own functions as messengers and my experience has borne these folk wisdoms out. There have been times when I was at a loss in a strange place, having no idea of what direction I should take to get where I wanted to be, when a bird—usually a crow or raven—would fly by. On following, I soon found myself exactly at the place I was looking for, though I had no Ordinance Survey map to guide me.

Sometimes, the feathered folk have played in tandem with the faeries to keep me in a particular place, for their own amusement, to get a message across, or to protect me from harm.

One midnight I was returning from the mountains north of San Francisco from a midwinter celebration (Imbolc, or Oimelc, in Gaelic. Lady Day to neo-pagans; St Brigid's Day, Candlemas to Catholics) at the house of my Celtic Studies teacher, and Kevin, my companion (later my husband), and I were both rather tired (to say nothing of having a little too much whiskey!) and anxious to get back to the city before the fog on the Golden Gate Bridge was impossibly thick. It transpired that we spent a good hour wandering in a circle on the same (noncircular) road in the mountains just outside Sebastapol, beset by white birds flying across our path, white rabbits likewise, and road signs turned ever toward the hills. We later discovered there had been an accident along our route, in which we would have been involved, had we not been delayed by these animal friends leading us merrily astray.

Thankfully, Kevin is a tolerant, open-minded soul, and though he was admittedly unnerved by our experience, he was not undone, for he had had his own experiences with faery horses (the puca) in Ireland the summer before. [He and his group of traveling companions were enticed to follow the puca across a bridge to Tir na nOg (the Celtic Valhalla). When they declined, the horses literally disappeared before their eyes.] But he learned then—or should have—that life with me was full of such little incidents.

When one considers all the lore of various birds—a direction being "as the crow flies"; the wisdom of owls; someone being as querulous as a jaybird, or flighty as a sparrow, to name just a few—we see that this tradition is submerged in the so-called subconscious of the population, to be revived in dreams and other alternative forms of reality. Jungian psychology is based upon this collective "unconscious" knowledge.

Though skeptics may take a jaundiced view of the way some people deal with their pets—or relate to the animal kingdom generally—who has not heard a dog howling outdoors on the death of a family member within, or a pet coming to comfort its owner during some grief? There is, always, whether we realise it or not, communication between us and other creatures. In times of stress, when this communication is most likely due to our openness, we do not ask how they know or how we know—we merely accept. The Lassie movies are a saccharin, but true, example of this acceptance. It is only later—when our supposedly rational mind has taken over again, that great HAL computer that we think makes us human, separates man from beast as some say—that we question and are perplexed.

But I would question why we should wish to be separated from our animal brethren. I have never wished to lose my rich and warm relationship with them. When I was feeling lonely as a child, I used to summon the creatures to me: birds, cats, whoever would come, for their companionship and they always lovingly came. I have at times agreed with Walt Whitman, who avowed that he would rather go and live with animals, for he found them to be truer to their essential nature than most men he knew.

To those who would question this Doctor Doolittle reality, this capacity of the animals to speak, I only pose balladeer John Denver's apt response: "How do you know they don't, just because they've never spoken to you?" All that is ever required to hear is a willingness to listen. Nobody, animals included, likes to natter on when he feels no one is listening to him.

If we accept that the world is alive all around us—and I do—and that time as we perceive it is only a convention of our current reality—as I always have, watching that little girl down there walk down a dusty road, knowing it was me and not-me at the same time—then we have a key to understanding the phenomenon that most people call ghosts.

Let me differentiate between what I mean by ghosts and the Hollywood variety: I have never encountered a poltergist, an alien, or an inhabitant of The Night of the Living Dead in my life. I have never been harmed. The intensity of the encounters I have had may have produced a few heart-thumping moments, but I never felt my mortal life endangered. By and large, the dead I have met with have been entirely decent people, bent upon solving some problem they had or merely going about their business in an everyday manner. Once in a while, they have simply dropped in to see how things are at their old haunts.

My family traveled around the country on summer holidays a good deal when I was a child, and places of historic interest were always at the top of the list, whether those were Civil War battlefields, mining towns in the Sierra Nevada, or points along the Oregon Trail. No matter where we went, I was always entertained, for always before my gaze was a panorama of what had gone on before. Not in some wishful, what-it-must-have-been-like way, but full of sound and, if applicable, fury. This immediate view of history in the making I get too in restored towns, which can make escorted tours a little disconcerting; they get in the way of what I'm watching. And when the tour guide's spiel is in direct conflict with what I see, it can be downright annoying.

One of my favourite ghosts was a lady I encountered in a restored mining town in California—Calico. It was the middle of a fine spring afternoon and she came out of a house on the main street of the town (there were only three). At liberty, I followed her about her business, to the bank, to the mercantile, to the dressmaker's. She stopped at one point on her return to chat with a neighbour over the picket fence, and I decided here to be on my way.

Walking along the street, I heard my name called and turned, to find the lady right behind me, her bonnet quivering in her astonishment, her blue eyes as round as saucers. The veil had been breached. Doubtless, she was wondering who this remarkable creature was wearing such peculiar clothes on the public street in Calico. My mother was waiting across the way, and this was truly a social occasion of the most painful ill-ease, so I said to her silently, "I'm not here," and dashed away. When I looked back, she was shaking her head, continuing on her walk.

Years later, while on a visit to Thomas Jefferson's home, Monticello, near Charlottesville, Virginia, I took the very first house tour one morning. As our group of four walked the familiar path from the sewing room into Mr. Jefferson's study, I espied a tall figure standing at the other end of the room at that early hour, his head bent into a book. He was half-dressed in shirtsleeves and waistcoat, with his hair hanging down undressed. He looked up as we entered, his hair falling across his face, and I was rewarded with the briefest of smiles before he went back to his book.

In the theatre this is known as breaking character; that is, deliberately interacting with the audience as an actor playing a role. It becomes a great inside joke, for in so doing one acknowledges that all of life is, in fact, merely a play we enact and not to take ourselves so deadly seriously. And Mr. Jefferson and I shared in that moment the great secret: that all the world's a stage, and men and women merely players.

And the play goes on without end. This is one show that will never close. Its run continues *ad infinitum*, adding and changing, ad libbing as we go; every actor's dream, for it is steady work, and we are all stars in this firmament.

Some see all our little individual souls as drops in the cosmic ocean, part of the whole, but sometimes distinguished. And some find this disconcerting. To be but an infinitesimal drop in a vast sea? What joy is there in that? But each drop is infinitely necessary to the whole and is a constant part of the whole. We all have our brief shining moments and even as King Arthur said of those drops in the ocean: "Some of them do shine, Pelle! How some of them do sparkle!"

We all can.

We all do.

Chapter Two

ॐ

School Days;
or, When You're Strange

For most children, the transition from nursery life with its natural rhythms and more or less carefree days to school life with its rules and demands is a challenging one. For ambitious young souls eager to get ahead in life (yuppies-in-training), it's the first crack at the game. For those with little essential life force, or Chi, as the Chinese say—dull podlings, to steal a term from Jim Henson's *Dark Crystal*—anything will do, though the curriculum beyond colouring Sparky the clown may place undue demands on their mental faculties. Then there are the ordinary Joes, who after the first week slide into the routine and seamlessly become part of the fabric of society at large. But for the organically weird, those born "different," members of Pugsleys Anonymous (my Addams Family-esque term for my group of weird friends), the entire scholastic experience, particularly if it is without the bounds of a comfy New Age alternative school, can be one long rude awakening and adjustment.

By school age, if one is to be enculturated at all, the basic patterns are set. This truth has been recognised by everyone from Attila the Hun and the Jesuits to modern pop psychologists. "Give me a boy till he's seven, and the man is mine for life!" rings the cry down through the ages, with variant results depending on the crier. Hitler is an excellent example of this, with avid followers who grew up in the Hitler Youth believing in his dogmas for the rest of their lives.

Most parents are less drastic in their enculturation than this, although some would say that Nintendo, Skippy peanut butter, and Kool-Aid are more insidious. (You are what you eat, and absorb, in all the ramifications of that.) In my own case, the outward symbols of enculturation were accepted, more or less. Usually less. That is

28

to say, I looked something like other children—if only through my mother's persistent effort—and ate more or less what they did, but I could not act like other children, nor think like them. That part of the programming was irretrievably skipped in the wiring of the DNA code. But until I went to school I never realized that I was different.

My mother was tolerant enough toward her weird child to let me dress up in whatever anachronistic get-ups I would—long peasant dresses with lace-up bodices, makeshift nun's habits, prairie dresses (one of my favourite pieces as a child was a prairie dress my mother cut down for me from an old print frock of hers; to this day I remember my rapture at finding it in the back of the sewing room closet, and my pure joy when she offered to make it over into whatever I wanted)—all labeled "dress-up play." My forays into the Otherworld were never questioned. It was all merely children's play. What had my mother to complain of? I knew all my numbers and letters, could read before I went to school; I was neat, quiet, and polite. What more could she ask? So it was that in kindergarten I stumbled on a shocking realization in the play yard that these other people, these kids, didn't know what I was talking about!

I was floored. How on earth was this possible? On earth indeed it was possible, and that was all the trouble. Having spent the first half-dozen years of my life not quite living on the same earth as others, but in a more, shall we say, expanded reality, I came out of my little theatre into the "real" world blinking like a mole in astonishment at mundane life. For I, like many Pisces children, had lived in a good and gentle world, inhabited by what have been euphemistically called "invisible playmates."

Through most of my childhood (and since!) I could be accused of not paying attention to what was going on around me, and I really was not. I was Other-focused, too busy reading people's states of being to put much mind to what they were saying, for what I was getting was far more meaningful and accurate. I used to hang out in the corner when my parents had card parties rather than playing outdoors with the guests' children because the adults were more entertaining. I could see in them all that they had been, and where they were currently.

It was a sorcerer's apprenticeship, and I attained my journeyman-ship fairly early, with such under-the-table insights (at below school age) as "Uncle Jim was a truly gentle, but harassed, soul. He was a sailor in heavy white trousers. . .His wife, Aunt Irma, is younger [soul-wise] and sour. Nothing would ever please her. She had been one of the bad monks who tortured people. They were together because she owed him, and he was to teach her gentleness. But she had warped his bright light with her constant whining and whining. They'd come back and try it again."

The next question, of course, was, "Well, how do these people think, if not as I do?" The answer to that was not long in coming, for kindergarten was a rude awakening to the ways of the world and the general effects of enculturation on our society upon "normal" children.

For I was, firstly, physically different and noticeable, being a redhead in southern California, the land of blonde and tanned. (Or Hispanic, or Oriental. I was the only redhead in the class until high school. Suffice it to say I was an oddity.) This caused me to be the subject of much unwonted, and unwanted, attention. Due to this notoriety, everything I did or said was remarked on more than it would have been had I been a raven or a jenny wren. There is an aspect of choice in this, and I freely admit it was not as bad as it might have been. I did not choose to be physically or mentally deformed—or challenged, as the current phrase runs—though I well might have under the circumstances. No, I merely chose to be a redhead and endure all the cultural assumptions that go with that. (I was not in fact a victim, a point which I am at pains to remind myself of even today. And I am very careful to whom, in the outside world, I make this "reminder," for it can prove a most unpopular notion! Nevertheless, when I was nine, such attention from schoolmates often felt like persecution.)

When I was very young, the others had not the words to define my difference from them. All they saw was a skinny, myopic, rather awkward little girl, of a solitary nature, extremely sensitive, who sang a lot, cried a lot, daydreamed, and talked—as they saw—to herself. Though I was when at home and in the wilds something of a tomboy, I was not much for team sports, preferring my ballet and other dance classes.

All this earned me a reputation for being aloof, a snob. They perceived that I viewed myself as better than they, which was not true. I viewed myself as different from them, and while it's true I hadn't much interest in their form of reality, I merely preferred mine, much as one would prefer vanilla to chocolate. I was not placing a value judgment on their way of being.

There were many who were more than willing to attempt to break through my perceived aloofness in handy fashion, with name-calling, hair-pulling, homework-destroying and after-school brawls; in the latter I would not endeavour to defend myself, though some sincere friends tried to teach me.

There was one girl who was particularly vicious. Her name was Gidget, and she was everything that was cool to be, and everything I was not: blonde, cute, popular, and clever (but not especially bright in the classroom). She took it into her head that I had something against her (maybe because I looked after her—so popular—wistfully) and would pick fights in the halls over some imagined slight or piece of gossip about her that had allegedly come from me, and she urged her coterie to do likewise. I never could understand why she hated me so. I had done nothing to her. Agelessness told me that she feared what she did not understand (me!) but the human heart felt the ostracism deeply. Her final wound was in enticing one of my best friends (so I *thought*) to join in the after-school harassment, a disillusionment from which I did not recover. To this day, I cherish the loyalty of friends.

It did not help that I *was* bright. Amongst the podlings and the bullies there were those who would alternately torment and court me—when they wanted help with their schoolwork; or in some cases to do the work for them. I was not unaware of their purposes in courting me, and privately resented it, but could not bring myself not to help them. Yet I was invariably crushed when my aid earned me no grace with them, and the next day or week I was again The Enemy.

Later, when their world view had broadened, they had words for my strangeness, words which were frightening in their resonances. From the time I was in middle school, I began to hear first whispers and then open taunts that I had what they called "the evil eye," that I was a witch.

It happened quite without my awareness. All I knew was that suddenly, any time I looked in someone's direction for longer than a moment, I would hear the whispers around me. I began to be seriously annoyed at this new form of harassment, for most of the while I was not even looking *at* the person, but through him. It came out into the open one balmy afternoon in late September when we were all settling into a map-reading course. The handsome football-player beau of my best friend turned around from his desk and stared at me with his large hazel eyes.

"I heard you are a witch," he said. The air went still around him, and I felt my face flush, my heart pounding in my ears. Half the room was looking on. Another set-up, dear God! He went on, "I heard you put a hex on _____. So, is it true?" He was grinning evilly.

"Leave me alone," I said, not looking at him. I made great pains to study the card map of New Jersey in front of me.

He persisted, facetiously cajoling, begging me to work some spell or the like. Red was before my gaze, the red of pain and fires. Old memories played in my mind, like a half-forgotten melody. In clarity of sight I now know there were at least three times I have been accused of practicing black arts; but then, they melded together in one image like stereoscopic pictures and I could not distinguish them one from another. The taunting was unbearable to me, who blushed at giving an answer in class, for the others about were watching. I never wanted their attention. Not that way. It was too like Before.

Ireland during the time of the Viking raids; Mediaeval England; the Hebrides under James VI (James I, if you're English); Ireland again in the Cromwellian period; the scenes of persecution were before my gaze again, with me facing down a group of angry villagers or other authority figures meting out their justice. I have always been a Seeker. Always been Different. And here it was again.

Finally, I steeled myself against tears and blushes and raised my eyes, gazing up at him balefully, with a raised eyebrow. "Leave me alone," I said again, slowly.

"It's true!" he crowed to whomever was listening. "She's a witch. She has the evil eye! Oh, she scares me. . ." Blah blah blah. I looked into the face of that puny little soul, who took pleasure in such tortures, and my heart turned over with hate. (I was only 13, after all.) It may merely have been the resonance of old times when I had been taken for a witch, but I hated this smart-mouthed jackeen, and everything he and his ilk could do to me. But I said nothing. Nothing at all. I went on, deciphering the map of New Jersey as best I could.

Yet he was not the worst of them. One even went so far as to check out a book on witchcraft from the school library in my name, a fact which I could verify as I worked in the library. When this rumour began to circulate, I confronted the party this time, to enquire the name of the book, and indeed found my name written there on the card, in a hand certainly not mine. That was the only instance in which I ever paid any mind to what was said of me. Nevertheless, I otherwise endured drubbings, mostly from girls who had insisted I was somehow maliciously intended toward them and their boyfriends. As if I would have anything to do with that lot!

How these children so instinctively knew all the catchwords and responses I do not know—Jung's collective unconscious, perhaps—but their response mirrors exactly those of witchcraft hysteria down through the centuries. They were sorely afraid of me, because I did seem to know things about them which no one else did (what their secret fears were, their anxieties, inadequacies; I could read the states of their souls in a glance) and fear is a powerful force. For my part, I lived in dread of being stoned, or attacked with shears or having other unpleasantnesses visited upon me, for I remembered these things, and had by this time been reading on that which I was accused of, and found my memories verified.

Since then, society's perception of witches and witch hunts in general (from ancient to modern times) have been a favourite study of mine, as it validates my experience in many lifetimes, and is not a bad cocktail party opener when asked what my hobbies are. People are still fascinated with the whole phenomenon, still do believe in witches and witchcraft. (Though Wiccans and other neo-pagans take exception to the general view of The Craft.)

There is a New England folksong which illustrates their response to me, as well as my own dread, as neatly as if it were written for my situation, though it concerns the real-life trial of Susanna Martin of Amesbury, Massachusetts, in 1692, during the witchcraft hysteria at Salem:

> *Susanna Martin was a witch who dwelt in Amesbury*
> *With brilliant eye and salty tongue she worked her sorcery*
> *And when into the judges' court the sheriffs brought her hither*
> *The lilacs drooped as she passed by, and then were seen to wither*
>
> *. . .The neighbours round swore to the truth of her Satanic powers*
> *That she could fly o'er land and stream and come dry shock or showers*
> *At night 'twas said she had appeared a cat oh fierce and mean*
> *The boys she devilled they had cried to keep their spirits clean*
>
> *The spectral evidence was weighed then stern the parson spoke*
> *"Thou shalt not suffer a witch to live, 'tis written in the Book."*
> *Susanna Martin so accused spake with flaming eyes,*

"I scorn these things for they are naught but filthy gossips' lies."
Now those bewitched they cried her out and loud their voice did ring
They saw a bird above her head an evil yellow thing
And so beneath the summer sky Susanna Martin died
And still in scorn she faced the rope, her comely head held high.

The last thing I wanted was to end up like poor Susanna Martin! And my experience had borne out that such things were still possible in this day and age, for pieces of my hair had been cut off (such are the charms of a public school education where this is allowed in the classroom!) and I was once threatened with fire. (This by one of the oh-so-tough secret-smoker girls, courtesy of Bic. The *real* tough girls, the biker chicks and drug addicts, accepted me blithely, and I thought often of Christ, hanging out with tax collectors and prostitutes. There was a reason, y'know. Acceptance!)

According to their minds, I was indeed a witch, for by that time—at the age of fifteen—I had picked up again many old skills: I had taught myself spinning and weaving and herbary, churning, dye craft, and so forth.

Such artsy-craftsy endeavours had always called to me, and upon seeing demonstrations of them at various fairs (or by my grandmother, who was very handy) the "thought" would come, "I can do that." And so I picked up and *did*. With spinning and weaving, I was given a small table loom when I was about nine, and proceeded to warp the thing and weave a sample piece in tabby (plain) weave without further instruction. It was only later that I picked up weaving books and checked out my technique. The same was true of spinning: I just picked up a drop spindle and did it. (And that is no simple endeavour.) When my husband indulged my sighing wish for a spinning wheel one Christmas, I likewise picked up a rolag of carded wool and spun, when I had laid hands on a wheel only a few times before at the Renaissance faires I worked. Before this, when we were in Ireland, I plucked stray wool off of fences in County Kerry and hand-spun it (sans drop-spindle) in the evening while visiting with our B&B hosts, and made up a small tapestry wool-sized skein. It is all very even and fine, free of slubs (or lumps to laypeople), for that was and is a requirement of mine: in the old days slubby wool was a sign of laziness and poor work, though it is fashionable now in yarn-crafting circles.

Herbary I took up entirely on my own. *Herbary,* like *midwifery,* was to me always a magical word, a magnet, familiar and comfortable. Walking into a health food shop as a pre-teen, I chanced upon John Lust's *Herb Book,* and the rest, as they say, is history. There were some discrepancies in his volume between the practices I "knew" and those he recommended (for instance, I remember most herbs being bruised in wine, decocted, or used as poultices, not taken in little gelatin capsules) but it was familiar enough to get me going again. I have quite a collection of herbals now, including some very old ones. It was in Nicholas Culpepper's *The English Physician; or The Compleat Herbal* (1652) that I found validation for my remembrance of herbs bruised in wine. Such has been my "research" this life, always backwards.

So my kitchen shelves became filled with little jars and bottles of herbs and tinctures I had put up myself, and the closets festooned with drying herbs culled from the wild reaches nearby; remedies for any ailment one might come across, and there were many jokes I never heard until much later about Kelly's witchy jars of "eye of newt" and "brown stuff" (tinctures). But the "brown stuff" worked, when nothing prescribed by the doctor would.

Being of northern European extraction on both sides of the family, my children have an allergy to citrus, as it is not something Celts and Vikings traditionally eat or therefore have the enzymes for, and our pediatrician could suggest nothing helpful for the distressing eczema from which my little ones suffered. Finally, in despair and disgust, I made up a concoction of dandelion, burdock, and yarrow, which cleared it up immediately. On our next visit, I informed our pedi of my success, for the edification of his other patients who likewise suffered, and he took down the information with thanks and many enquiries as to why exactly it worked, which I could supply in suitable allopathic terms. Score one for traditional medicine! It has been an aim of mine since to meld traditional and modern medical practices, and I have striven to do so in my midwifery work, for both disciplines have their places and their strengths, and I am a great believer in the Middle Path. (Though I do, I confess, still prefer willow bark to aspirin!)

Churning, like preserving, pickling, and several forms of needlecraft, I learned from my adoptive grandmother in northwestern Illinois, whence I was sent in the summers, to "the farm," to visit assorted relatives. She was a great large and cheerful woman, everyone's stereotypical grandmother, who baked cherry pies from scratch and made watermelon pickles in the summer, and I bless her memory. She was, for her part, very glad of her little granddaughter who showed such an interest in old-timey stuff.

Sewing I learned from my mother, who made most of my clothes as a child, but my bent was different from hers; mine was always for "old stuff," and still is. Anything ethnic or vintage is fair game for my needle, from English (or, Welsh!) smocks to Indian cholis. I do use a sewing machine, but it is sitting cross-legged on the floor stitching by hand that I prefer, for it hearkens me back to France in the late 13th century, when I spent a very short life as a tailor; and to mid 19th-century Kansas, when I was a dressmaker (though not much else was pleasant about that life); and to a particular lifetime in 18th-century Virginia, when my life was much taken up with sewing, both for my little family and for our larger black family, for I was then the mistress of a large (but not especially prosperous) plantation in central Virginia.

All the things I "knew," and undertook, have resonances from domestic life and former occupations, and I undertook them fairly early in my life. If I am not a Mozart, composing harpsichord pieces at age five, then I am at least adept at these "old-timey" arts, which serve me in right good stead. I would never be undone if faced with a lack of modern amenities due to a power outage or a snowstorm, which is more than may be said for most city-bred folk.

But to my high-school compatriots I was beyond the beyonds, for I knew the phases of the moon and the right time for engaging in various activities (the old *Farmer's Almanack* being a dear friend.) Moreover, I wore strange clothes: cloaks for instance, or any odd bit of vintage or reproduction or ethnic garb that struck my fancy. To any rational mind, such actions would be merely those of a craftsperson, re-enactor, or eccentric (or possible all three at once), but their view of the world was not yet sufficiently broad to encompass such possibilities easily.

My adoptive family, which by high school was comprised of my father and my sister and her children (for my adoptive mother had died), thought I was a complete nut with my inexplicable yearnings for things past. Didn't I want to wear polyester pantsuits like every other fashionable young girl? Didn't I want to listen to the Bee Gees, lie out in the sun, et cetera? I most assuredly did not! I had no wish to participate in their version of reality.

My father complained once of my 1930s-style brown summer frock, "What do you want to wear that old stuff for? It looks trashy." Here he was showing his biases, for he grew up during the Depression, and anything handmade was to him home-made, therefore inferior to store-bought goods, and I'm sure the style of the dress hearkened him back to days of wondering where the next meal was coming from. Yet even he had a penchant for nostalgia: he lugged home from one of our jaunts to Illinois several old milk tins, oil lamps, and yard pumps, which had been rattling around his mother's basement for years unregarded. The milk tins he sold for a handsome price; the oil lamps he filled and then refused to let anyone—mostly me—use because they were "special"; and the yard pumps he connected to hoses outdoors to let us children play in. (And all I could think of was Helen Keller and "wah-wah," and I had flashes of lugging water to a sod house; shades of the 19th century and my life out on the Kansas prairie.)

In those days I struggled mightily with the wherefores of my situation. How was it that I was so afflicted? Why would they not just let me be the way I was, as I let them? I was not vying for converts to my world view. Such understand would only come later when I had freed myself from that tiny world, and come to know that there were others likewise seeking to understand. But o! would that I had seen the film *Highlander* then, for it would have relieved my mind greatly.

For in that film, protagonist Connor MacLeod is an immortal who has just been informed by one of his ilk of his true nature. This after being driven from his home by angry villagers, who were incensed that he did not die of battle wounds and called him a devil. Shocked at the news and stunned by his experience, Connor asks his teacher how it could have happened. The teacher responds, "Why does the sun come up? And are the stars merely pinholes in the curtain of night? Who knows! But I do know this: because you were born different, men will fear you, try to drive you away, like the people of your village."

The philosophic essence of the teacher's response bears examination: that indisputably, there are those who have come here to exist in a different way from the bulk of humanity, to see beyond mere matter to spirit, to be one with everything that is. It is, possibly, the culmination of human experience. In any case, it hurts. But it is, nevertheless, merely the way of things, part of nature.

At the end of the film when Connor has won the prize for which all have struggled and fought throughout, he says: "It's like a whirlwind inside my head. If I concentrate, I can hear what people are thinking all over the world—presidents, scientists, diplomats, and I can help them understand each other. . .You never prepared me for that. . ."

His teacher responds with a laugh. "Patience, Highlander! It will take time. You are generations being born and dying. You are at one with all living things. Each man's thoughts and dreams are yours to know. You have power beyond imagination. Use it wisely my friend. Don't lose your head."

What, after all, is this much-sought-after Prize? Why, mortal life of course! The chance to be here upon this watery little planet; to live, to love, to have children, to grow old. And those who live beyond the veil realize what a blessing it is to be able to play in the halls of history such roles as mankind devises for its amusement.

My salvation in society during my difficult time in school—and possibly the only reason I did not become entirely anti-social—was the theatre, the public stage. From dancing, I took up acting at the age of fourteen and found a home amongst the bohemian artists, greasepaint, and musty costumes. Here fancy was not merely tolerated, but encouraged, and nobody questioned how I came by what I knew, for creating a role is done mostly from intuition and experience. Actors being all misfits in some way from "real life," I was no more or less strange than anyone else, and the over-riding tolerance of the theatre for others' peculiarities was a balm for what I was suffering on the outside. Here I was teased, but it was with affection and not malice, and I yielded, blooming, giving as good as I got.

The performing life became a launching point for me as well as a refuge, for I saw in it that I was not in fact as unfit for life as I had begun to think; that I would make for myself a way, a place, that had no part of society's push to be "normal." I had no wish for the dead boredom of the nine-to-five workaday world with its mania for owning things for owning's sake. I realized that I was not necessarily subject to what I viewed as slavery, and took a radical step toward fulfilling my own destiny: I took (and passed) the general proficiency examination and left high school at the age of sixteen for college.

I was warned off this by nearly everyone I knew, as I have been warned off everything my heart said was right since by those well-meaning people around me who are content with the everyday path. Everyone argued patience. They tempted me with visions of graduation ceremonies, senior year, and senior proms. But what charms had such for me, who had never been accepted by the bulk of my contemporaries there, had never dated anyone from the school? There was no kinship for the outsider, beyond a remarkable few, and with those I could maintain contact. In the broader world I would find greater acceptance of what I was, and a space in which to create that which I was becoming. So I left, and have never regretted it a day or an hour.

I was vindicated in my knowing and my beliefs, for almost immediately I came into contact with a young woman with the same understanding as I, who had endured much the same experience of "differentness," of being outside her society. I met this dear sister, Wendy (named for Wendy Darling in *Peter and Wendy*, by J.M. Barrie), in the green room of the theatre where we both worked in college; an appropriate metaphor for our reality.

For those of you not immersed in backstage life, the green room is the general meeting room of the theatre, where actors hang out when they are not onstage, and mostly they let it all hang out there. A few years ago, my spirit guide, Irene, and the rest of my entity-mates "up there" (disembodied), used the image of the green room to me for their existence, knowing I would immediately get it. They said,

> You would ask us of what we do with our "time" here. First of all, as you are aware, we do not experience "time" in the way that you perceive it, although we do have a sense of progression, of evolution. That caveat given, we will use your words and concepts so that you understand us, but know that our words are only so you understand us, and are in no way meant to be taken literally. We spend about forty percent of our "time" in analyzing and re-enacting life scenes for those who have departed the physical plane, to help them fit their experience into the whole of their life-span and understand it, much as in improvisational theatre. Approximately thirty percent of our "time" is spent in actual teaching such as this, and the rest is dedicated to what you would call "hanging around." Do not envision angels with harps and clouds here, for that is not our reality. We assure you that we can and do have a good time playing. Your equivalent would be actors in the green room during the run of a show. We have our own business to discuss, but we keep an eye on the stage—the physical plane in this case, and when someone of you deviates from their planned course, or otherwise experiences a difficulty, we all as actors will come and watch, and "mouth the cues" if you will. You are never alone. We are always pulling for you.

The image they gave me was of the cast of *Hamlet* lounging about the tatty sofas, smoking cigarettes and gossiping. Once in a while someone would cock an ear to the action onstage. If somebody fluffed a line, they would all gather round the wings to watch how Rosencrantz or Gildenstern got themselves out of this one, and would cue them the lines in a loud stage whisper ala vaudeville. I thought, "Gee, thanks guys," for they were obviously having a laugh at the *ad libbing* going on down here "onstage." But it was not with malice, for they had all "been there"; we are all actors together.

So it was with my friend Wendy. There was an instant recognition, and a compulsion to get to know one another. Neither of us was hard to miss. In those days, she sported the garb of Dr. Who, the British science fiction hero, in his incarnation as the actor Tom Baker, with the mile-long scarf, slouch hat, long woolen coat and all. I was in my prairie period, and wore ballet tights under everything, for I was dancing then and almost never had time to change between the studio and the theatre. (This was a great joke amongst the theatre-rats, and for Christmas one year one of the girls made me a large effigy of myself, dressed in a prairie dress with ballet togs underneath.)

The meeting with Wendy was suspiciously inauspicious. Our glances met as we hurried past one another on our backstage business—as it turned out we were both in the costuming class for Theatre Design—and we immediately understood that neither of us was ordinary, though we might live outwardly ordinary lives; that the path for us was not that lauded in fashion magazines. We share a deep, mystical understanding of what may be called the occult, and a profound love of the land. This knowledge of one another we gleaned through the long hours in the costume shop or backstage during shows, for we were the flying monkeys of the place, doing the bidding of wicked witch (costume mistress). We had not spent huge amounts of time in each other's company in past lives, but we made up for it in this life, in those long days and nights in the bowels of Burnight Theatre.

I owe Wendy a great debt, for she facilitated illumination of my fascination (inexplicable to my adoptive family) with the Celts. It was in her house that I first heard the music of the Irish band, the Chieftains. It was there that I heard "O'Carolan's Welcome," which was written down in the 18th century, but based on a traditional tune.

. . .And on that hearing found myself both watching the scene and standing on a road in County Clare, Ireland, in the 1650s. It was falling dusk, and I was waiting for my husband to return from Ennis Town, and was anxious, because I had had a vision that he would not return, had begged him not to go. He never did return alive, but was killed in the town by Cromwell's soldiers. I was a strong-minded woman then, a midwife who also ran a shebeen—an illegal public house. All this I knew in a moment. I saw Lelia—for such was her name, the Gaelic for Elizabeth—clearly, knew her life's history in broad strokes.

Nearly ten years later, I found myself on that road in County Clare at dusk when I was in Ireland doing fieldwork for my thesis. I grabbed my husband's arm. He maintains that I shouted "Stop! That's it!" at the top of my voice. All I knew was that I was overcome with a sense of *deja vu*. We had passed the spot a couple of times, and I always eyed the derelict ancient house with the roof beam fallen in. But something about the quality of light was right at that moment. It was the house the Tipperary thatcher John Larkin had built with his own hands. Lelia's husband. Lelia's house.

I got out of the car, shuddering with cold—my body's infallible truth meter—and stood on the road in the very spot I had done 330 years before, and had seen again in my dear friend's house. The mountains beyond, the curve of the road, the ruined church up on the hill, they were all the same.

I could not go into the house, could not tear the veil then, (though I would do it now). But I took a small stone from the door lintel of my house that John Larkin built for us with his own hands in a single day, in the blustery cold of West Clare before Samhain (Hallowe'en), so that we could claim it free of rates and rent, according to the custom of the time and place. I have that stone yet, tucked away with other such treasures, for it is more to me than some old rock. It is confirmation of the true reality. Validation.

All this was possible due to my dear friend. I facilitated things for her too, just by being true to who I was. I opened up her mind to the nature of time, and helped her put a few of her relationships into perspective.

Though compatible in many ways—both practicing a form of natural religion—we are not identical. Her special focus has been the native peoples here, as well as her Celtic forbears; mine the "other" Indians—from India—and my Celts likewise. We balance each other nicely, our paths mirroring, each having a common knowledge and strengths for the other's deficiency. Proof enough that we do not have to be just the same as someone else for a relationship to work.

Later, at the university from which I took my degree, I met a young woman who had shared my "witch" experience. She too, was fey-looking: tall and blonde and very thin with enormous hazel eyes; she too, wore cloaks and vintage clothes and had been a theatre rat. She too lived amidst poetry and candles and stitchery. She too, in high school, had had "witch!" whispered after her as she passed by, had been drubbed and persecuted. But she endured it—with great pain I will say, as she was a devout Catholic.

She was not hard to meet, either. I had seen her about campus, in her long pink cloak, but was too shy to speak to her. Then she turned up in an English course of mine on Image, Metaphor and Symbol, and I swallowed my shyness and went to speak to this enchanting creature. Our mutual experience we hardly ever spoke of, but it was a silent bond between us. We instead spent many a pleasant hour idling in the halls of the past, in a place of gentility, grace, and beauty (though she could be profoundly practical: she singlehandedly rebuilt the engine of her 1970s VW bus). When she revealed to me her own experience of persecution I was at heart not surprised, but was moved to compassion and began to truly perceive how common an experience mine truly was.

"See," my friends upstairs in the Green Room seemed to be saying, "you are not so alone, little sister. There are many of your coterie."

Since beginning this book, that perception has been validated over and over again. Recently while I was interviewing my midwifery partner, her roommate came into the kitchen where we sat cozily with a pot of tea and chimed into our conversation with great enthusiasm: "Oh, I had that too! No one could ever see my kachinas in the clouds or my leprechaun friend, and I wondered why." Anytime my experience is spoken of—generally by a facilitating friend—I hear the same response: "That happened to me, too!" Plainly, those of us of like minds, souls, and experience are gathering together, reinforcing one another.

The most extreme case of "differentness" I have come across, the most assured member of Pugsleys Anonymous (as I affectionately call my little circle of weird compatriots), is my aforementioned friend and midwifery partner. Cathleen's experience bears examination due to its complexity, which on any level of reality is fascinating.

She was born into what is known in the Catholic Church as a mixed marriage, her mother being Catholic and her father a Southern Baptist from Oklahoma (such mixing at that time being frowned upon by the Church, as it implies less than a staunch adherence to the Faith—as proved true in her parents' case) and she was duly christened in the Church according to the precepts of that time; only, as she laments, to have her parents become Jehovah's Witnesses when she was small. This she long regarded as an unforeseen change of plans, though she since admits that she must have agreed to it somewhere.

She was reared to see herself as different from the rest of society, in the world but not of it, chosen but not special. She was indeed set apart from her contemporaries, more profoundly than I was, for there were restrictions of dress and manner and belief to which I was not subject.

But even within that society she was strange, and it caused her no little pain to be doubly unacceptable. For she saw things no one else did; had knowledge of history for which her everyday experience had no explanation; and longed for the material culture of societies with which she had had no contact.

She tells the story of living across from San Francisco's oldest church, the Basilica of Mission Dolores, and daily watching the nuns move about their business, and of the longing she had to, as she says, "just go and hang out with them." This might have been understandable from a Catholic child, but to the Witnesses (as they call themselves) Catholics were the anti-Christ and she was told frightening tales against entering that world. It was not, in fact, until we had known each other for some time that she ventured into that holy place, though she had lived in the city forty years.

Meanwhile, she had collected the material trappings of Catholicism, much to her family's dismay. Rosary beads, crucifixes, books of hours, Gregorian chant, all call to her from without her current experience. Once, inexplicably to all, she showed up at a Hallowe'en party as a 13th-century French nun. The pull of the past was that strong and specific.

She has told of a vision that came to her as a child of lying face-down on the cold stone of the nave of a church, as a penance for some fault. Her description of the place, the reasons for the penance, and the process were as vivid as the annals of the saints, and as accurate, though she has no knowledge of such matters in her everyday reality. Her experience stands as a window on the past; and it is but one of many such. Other, more ancient places call also: India, Burma, Egypt, Syria, Rome.

All these spring from a childhood of wondering. Grown-ups never seemed to do anything, she said. Why were we here and where were we all going? Was it truly as her church elders said, that so many people were evil and would perish in horrible fashion? And if so, how could one love such a God? Who was God? What did he look like? And whence did God start?

I had such questions myself as a child. Every person I have talked to who saw themselves as different as a child admits to them. There is always a profound curiosity of unseen things. When I was a child, I particularly wanted to be dead, for the dead were with God, so I was told, and to my mind knew everything. I wanted answers to my thousand questions. If I were dead I would know the answers. . .I never stopped to question the continuance of life afterward.

My friend was taught a catechism of fear (unlike heathen me who was reared with no official religion, though I had plenty of Catholic friends to supply it, taking me to Mass, teaching me prayers and such), in that after death there was nothing. The void. Eternal blackness. The long sleep. Now, Cathleen had some pretty far-out experiences when she was asleep and thought everyone else did, too, so that was a fine idea, until she began to learn that what she was experiencing was, according to her church elders, "of the devil." Anything instinctive was Satanic.

For a child who regularly saw faces in objects, saw ghosts, and felt presences, this was a hell indeed, for, according to the church elders, had she been so foolish as to tell them, this was witchcraft. And because she was not demure, she had already been taught to see herself as a wicked person.

But even with all this, her sense was that "it shouldn't be this hard. . .all these rules. . .to be a person. God knows what's inside me, that I'm a good person, even if these people don't."

She had her rebellion against her religious training in due course, even as I did against my persecutors, and on entering the wide world discovered that religion, as John Donne would have it, was not a dampe.

If someone asked me for a profile of the typical experience of an organically weird child, I would say there is:

- A strong sense of self
- A sense of isolation or solitude
- No desire to experience accepted reality
- Regular occurrences of precognition, *deja vu*, astral travel, telepathy, and past-life recall
- Regular, if minor, episodes of melancholy tempered with great joy
- Often artistic sensibilities, if not actual talent
- Greater comforts (in school) with adults than other children

- Some form of external persecution
- Profound, if unorthodox, spirituality

This list only holds, of course, for our Western culture, where such uncanny experiences as *deja vu* and astral travel are viewed with great suspicion and disdain. Those in Eastern or other traditional cultures will find their experiences varying according to the latitude of their culture. Those who seek answers to the Eastern experience of the organically weird may turn to the lists of books and movies in the Appendix. For the rest of you: sail on, sojourner!

Chapter Three

ॐ

". . .the smithy of my soul"; or Odysseus

The quote above is from James Joyce, who wrote of his work that he had "forged within the smithy of my soul the uncreated conscience of my race." The words have always struck home with me, and I have the profoundest respect for Jimmy, though most people find him tedious and self-important (as did many in Dublin at the time, as I have firsthand reason to know). Such is the hazard of telling it like you see it. Just look at what they did to Socrates!

Joyce is the perfect launching point for my experiences once I moved to San Francisco, for there, indeed, everything began happening at once, and if things were to make any sense at all, they had to be viewed by their interior logic and no other, else they would be all so much nonsense.

To catch you up on how I got from southern California to northern California (where I felt much more at home), it is necessary to go back to college theatre life, then take a slight detour to Virginia between whiles, as I did.

While yet in the LA 'burbs, I was strongly drawn to the Catholic Church (unsurprising as I have spent several lifetimes as a monk in England or France). I had wanted my whole life to convert but was thwarted in this by my father, who, though he had no religion himself, was highly anti-Catholic. (It had been my mother who allowed me to go to Mass and all with my friends.) I remember well when I was thirteen we went to Catalina Island on a day jaunt, and with money I had won in a raffle I was allowed to buy "whatever I wanted." Well, "whatever" did not happen to include the rosary of blue aurora borealis beads I chose. My father had fits and I was in tears, until the family friend who was with us took him aside and said quietly, "It's her money. It's not hurting anything. Let her have them. It's good for the child to have religion." How grateful I was to Jessie for her words! So I had my rosary, and it was (and is) cherished.

My father's tolerance of my desire was rather stretched when I announced that I wished to become a nun (I was about sixteen at this time). I had done much reading on the Poor Clares—a very strict cloistered order, who still wore the old medieval habits and had a vow of silence—and I wanted very much to give my life over to such service to God. Dad absolutely hit the roof. "You aren't even Catholic!" he railed.

"No," I said quietly, "but I will be. I can do that now." For I had looked into the process of conversion while at Mass, and Wendy's father, a permanent deacon, had confirmed that I was indeed old enough.

Obviously, I did not become a nun, but I did convert; Wendy's father was the one who welcomed me into the Church, and she stood as my sponsor both at my baptism and confirmation. I spent six months taking instruction from an Irish priest from County Meath (and to this day I recite the Creed in the Irish manner), and on my eighteenth birthday, St. Patrick's Day, I had my dearest wish. A few weeks later, at Easter, I had my confirmation, taking as my patron the first American saint, beatified in 1963, my birth year, and canonized in 1975: Elizabeth Bayley Seton, Mother Seton, born in 1774.

She was also a convert, a former New York belle who lost her husband to consumption (TB) in Italy, and there found comfort in the Church. She had several children, but in spite of this became an abbess and the founder of the parochial school system in America. Her prayer runs:

> *Lord God,*
> *you blessed Elizabeth Ann Seton*
> *with gifts of grace*
> *as wife and mother,*
> *educator and foundress,*
> *that she might spend her life*
> *in service to your people*
> *Through her example*
> *and prayers,*
> *may we learn to express*
> *our love for you*
> *in love for one another*

There being no coincidences in life, I found that when I moved into the parish in San Francisco where I spent ten years, where Kevin and I were married, there was a window with her likeness and story depicted. And my beloved Mother Seton was the Elizabeth of St. Elizabeth's Maternity Home, where I worked with teenaged mothers, where I met Cathleen; the sisters who operated it were of the order Mother Seton founded.

While still in college in southern California, I felt the need to come to Virginia. I wanted to work in the costume department at Colonial Williamsburg and had enough experience with my theatre training to get in at least as an apprentice. CW required a personal interview, so I planned to come for two weeks to do it during the Easter break. Two weeks stretched into five months, as no job opened up in the Costume Design Center, and I was enticed by one possible job after another as various costumed interpreters, including one at the bakery at the Raleigh Tavern, which would have put my hearth cookery skills to use.

But at every turn, I was told that the job had been given to someone "inside," and that I had excellent skills, that "if there were another position, we would hire you." It was a bitter pill. I would have starved had it not been for the intercession of kindly friends, for there was no job to be had no where, no how. I lived on my student Social Security allowance (courtesy of my mother), which covered my rent and utilities and was left with fifteen dollars to spare. Those were lean times at the John Yancy with the hot and cold running cockroaches! I left the lights and air conditioning on all the time, as I had heard the creepy-crawlies liked neither. (It's a lie.)

This was sensory overload, a form of torture, and I had empathy for the hunger strikers in Belfast, whose travails I daily followed in the papers, for it kept me sane. It was comforting to know that somewhere in the world, there was someone—ten someones— worse off than I.

This resonance, of Ireland, was fairly strong and growing stronger all the while, though I knew not why at the time. I would discover why when I came to San Francisco, but that was six months in the future. At the time, I knew only that there were ten men suffering indignity and death for want of the right to wear their own clothing and to be treated with the dignity supposed to be accorded to political prisoners under the articles of the Geneva Convention.

I took the plight of the hunger strikers as a barometer of my own situation. If they were allowed to die, then surely there was no hope for me either, in Virginia. The day Bobby Sands died, 5 May, 1981,

I went home from looking at the papers in the public library and wept for an hour, for Bobby—who was a fine poet and family man—and for myself. I cursed Margaret Thatcher and the whole British government. As with the Fenians in the 19th century, an unfair imprisonment made a lifelong rebel out of one who was formerly indifferent. I cursed Colonial Williamsburg and their insular policies. It was a black day. (I have often wondered how much the resonance of that day—5 May—affects matters, for my second son, Cian, was born then, and he has been afflicted with melancholy from birth. What rough beast, to plagiarize Yeats, slouches toward Bethlehem from that fateful day? What ripples did that event unleash upon the world? Perhaps it is too soon to tell.)

There were other resonances operating here in Virginia, which were the true cause of my coming here in the first place. One was that it was my birthplace in the incarnation in the 19th century that ended in Kansas. But the big draw was that it was the home I knew in the late 18th century. Then, I was born in Charles City County, not far from Williamsburg, the eldest daughter of a Welsh emigrant from Lancashire. My name was Martha Wayles. To my family and justly famous second husband I was known as Patty. That second husband was also the descendant of Welsh emigrants; he was born in Albemarle (then Goochland) County. His name was Thomas Jefferson.

My earliest memory of that life sprang from a seeming innocuous visit to Disneyland with my uncle at age five. We stood in their theatre-in-the-round, taking in the trip through these glorious United States. I do not recall what came before or after, so galvanizing was the experience, but suddenly, I found myself on Duke of Gloucester Street—the main street in the historic area—and I was shaking with cold. *I know this place!!!!*

I saw, felt, knew myself to be a little woman with curly dark-red hair. Patty was her name, and she was as sweet and gracious as she was vivacious. She was married, and her husband was a tall, sandy-haired fellow. She loved to come to town because it meant visiting people, and it was a rare occurrence. Oh, I knew Williamsburg! And loved it. I came back to the theatre with a jolt, verging almost on panic, when the camera moved on. *Wait! Go back! I KNOW that place! Williamsburg. . ..*

From that time I would set upon all folks from Virginia, and God help them if they were from Williamsburg, or anywhere that sounded vaguely like it. (When I was six, I plagued a neighbour for a good hour, insisting that she was funning me, insisting that she tell me the truth, because I discovered she was from Walsomburg. How disappointing to learn it was in Colorado!)

Thomas Jefferson was always a draw. I *knew* him, who he was, inside. He and his little beloved wife. Inexplicable things would come to me about them. How did I know, for instance, that she had a sister named Anne? When I was old enough to read Thomas's biographer Dumas Malone, I discovered that there was an Anne among John Wayles' quartet of lovely daughters. But that was in high school, and the memory came when I was in grammar school.

I never cared much for his life beyond Patty's death. Oh, I read of it, knew its course, but my real interest pretty much died with her. Likewise, the domestic life at Monticello, not his career, was my primary focus.

Then, when I was first in college, Fawn Brodie's *Intimate History* was put in my way. I happened on it in the new book section of our college library and immediately sat down on the floor with it. At last! What I was looking for!

I turned to the index. Martha Wayles Jefferson. How many entries were under her name was always my test of the book's worth. But I was so incensed by what I read that I threw the book down (which earned me no points with the librarian). I took especial exception to the deathbed scene wherein Mrs J is supposed to have made Thomas promise never to marry again. *It didn't happen that way! I have been misquoted!* was what came through my mind. Many other memories were to come to the fore, in protest, as I read Ms. Brodie's book. Meanwhile, I sang the part of Martha in *1776*, and it was all-too-comfortable.

So I found myself called to Virginia, to re-experience, in my long and lonely hours, the places I had known. I took long walks in the woods, wandered the Historic Area like the shade I was becoming, and the memories flooded in. I met with Thomas everywhere, in the places we had known. And sweet it was. Most of the memories were of utterly mundane things that—I thought—no one would care about. I kept them to myself. With my experience of school, the last thing I wanted to do was to *give* people a reason to persecute me, and saying "I was married to Thomas Jefferson in a past life" would certainly open me up to ridicule. Besides this, it conflicted with orthodox Catholic dogma, which was a great problem for me. I didn't know how to reconcile matters in my mind, so shelved the resonances of Patty for the nonce. When in doubt, avoid the whole subject.

My jobless situation forced me to return to California, and I had a real desire, which was not predicated on escaping the pressures of so-called real life, to get back to school. I wanted to earn my degree. But there was there waiting for me another upheaval which would take me from my native place to San Francisco, where destiny waited. (I remarked to Wendy, of San Francisco, "I'll find my destiny there." I am convinced that the universe is set up to make us eat such thoughtlessly blurted words, for I had no idea at the time how true they would be. I had a general sense of moment, even of great moment, but the details evaded me.)

For, in addition to the Irish Question and that of my academic future, there was one which had plagued me since I was seven: who was my natural mother, and did she miss me, love me? What was she like? Was I like her, like my father? The time had come for me to search out the answers.

I had a general idea of her, based on nothing material, by which I mean that my adoptive parents had told me nothing (though they had the information I required in a strongbox in their room, I later discovered.) I thought of her as blonde, cool, listening to Joan Baez and Bob Dylan in coffeehouses with my father. (This was more a resonance of my own most immediate past life as a beatnik artist-cum-cocaine addict in Liverpool, but I didn't know that at the time.) Nevertheless, I was determined to know the material facts, so I contacted ALMA, the Adoptees Liberty Movement Association, a group which helps families such as mine reconnect with one another. A week afterward, my grandmother in San Francisco contacted the same group and viola! about a week later I found two letters from San Francisco in my mailbox.

I had been to San Francisco only once, when I was nine, as the last leg of a long jaunt around the country. My foremost memories are of eating spaghetti at Alioto's on Fisherman's Wharf (and being chided for eating pasta at the most famous fish restaurant in San Fran), and being completely enchanted with a shirtless, long-haired man who was unloading goods from a truck at the back of a shop.

That February afternoon, I came in from work to find my sister and cousin sitting in the kitchen discussing soap operas. Ignoring their chat, I sifted through the mail and came upon the two tan envelopes. My heart was thudding in my ears, and I ran chills. I knew no one in San Francisco. I stood for a long time, divining the sender and contents, instead of opening them, as any normal person would do. *My god, it's from her!*

I opened the letters carefully, and found them to be from my grandmother, with pictures and all. Gently, she informed me that my mother had died in 1972 (when I was nine, at about the time I was in SF) but that she had loved me very much and it hurt her deeply to have to give me up.

My ears were ringing, and I must have been pale, because my cousin asked me what the matter was. Stunned, I mumbled the contents of the letter. But my mind was shouting *She Loved Me! She Loved Me!* until it became a mantra, the Beatles song ("She Loves You"), reality.

For when it was near my seventh birthday, I went to my mother where she was sewing and asked her a fateful question which changed my life and interior being to a degree almost incomprehensible. Around my birthday, I always wondered about my mother, and whether she thought of me too, on my special day. But that year, I took courage in hand, and asked, "Who was my real mother and what was she like?" And my poor mother, who had wanted me so much—with her own sad history of surgery and loss—replied, "She wasn't your real mother. She didn't love you enough to keep you."

As a mother myself, I know the place from which my mother spoke, but it took me until I had my own children to forgive her, for her words crushed me entirely and threw me into doubt about my lovability, a complex from which I yet suffer in times of stress.

Thus my grandmother's words were affirming, and the first step—at age nineteen—on the road to recovery, to learning to love myself, which is the basis of enlightenment and freedom from the cycle of rebirth. (Thank you, Nana. Namaste.)

I went for a visit, and while there decided to enroll in San Francisco State University, as they had good English, History, Theatre, and Creative Writing Departments—and one of the on-campus groups was Students For A United Ireland. The threads in the tapestry were beginning to weave together. My grandparents offered to let me stay at their house while I was in school. I accepted, and moved in June. Just in time for the summer session. During which time my future husband Kevin was abroad in Ireland with our teacher, Laurie Fadave. Soon, life would begin to resemble an episode of "The Twilight Zone," or any page out of *Finnegan's Wake*.

It did not take long. In the long lazy days between the summer session and the fall term, I went with my grandmother to Sunday devotions, she to her church (the Quaker meetinghouse) and I to mine. They were not far apart, and she would drop me off at St. Monica's, and I would after Mass walk down to the Friends' Center in time for silent meeting.

One day, the Mass was especially illuminating.

It was the interior of the church which triggered the scene, for it was as many a Jesuit church anywhere in the world, and specifically identical to the one in Gardiner street in Dublin I would visit four years in the future—the very church I had worshipped in, if you can call it that, in the 1910s. But all that was before me yet.

What I knew that Sunday morning was only a weird sense of unreality as the Mass began, a sort of shimmering faintness which had nothing to do with the regulation of a morning fast. By the middle of the Mass, I began to find myself in two places at once, existing in a double-exposure or a hologram. I was Kelly standing in St. Monica's in San Francisco, and at the same time a tall, dark-haired, very pregnant woman in a grey-blue frock and broad-brimmed blue velvet hat. Beside me was a tall, redheaded, bespectacled man in salt-and-pepper tweeds and a little redheaded boy. Our son. I was annoyed with the Mass, uncomfortable in my tight shoes, irritated at being in public so very pregnant, put out at my husband, with whom I had fought that morning. The smell of incense was cloying, sickening, so sickening I—thought—I—would. . .faint.

And I did. In 1912, and 1982. That was the first time I met Molly.

She came up in my consciousness again when the fall term began. I would be walking across the lawn of the quadrangle and her image would be before me: standing before a window in a white dress, waving down to someone. M. M something. Her name. But I couldn't get it. Then she turned from the window at a noise—a man came in the room at the opposite door, and I saw her face. She was aristocratic and beautiful with fine bones and pale grey eyes. West of Ireland grey eyes.

Meanwhile, I was taking up Celtic studies and getting involved with the local Irish community, both of which would feature in my getting who this woman was, and what she meant to me, and what the connection was to my fainting episode of the summer.

I was due to meet a man from the Irish Forum at one of their lectures, given this time by the Reverend Martin Smythe, a high-ranking Ulster Unionist. The Irish Forum sponsored such lectures in an effort at dialogue between the factions, and the man I was to meet was a died-in-the-wool-Republican, whose father had been killed before his eyes in 1921 by the notorious Black and Tans. (A makeshift martial law force culled from British prisons to put down the Irish rebellion. They were largely murderers and rapists, and not your decent ordinary criminals, such as thieves or army deserters.) There were many in the audience whose sympathy did not exactly run with the speaker, I among them.

I stepped off the elevator, my mind all on the old man, and there before me, with his back to me, was a dark-haired young man in an Aran sweater. I felt not a chill this time, but an electric shock. *I know you!*

He turned around. He had straight hair that fell in his eyes, a mustache, and great pale-blue eyes. A wash of pure rage went through me. *How dare you look like HIM!* I had no idea what this meant, only that I was compelled and repelled by this man. I had to know him.

When the call came for the lecture to begin, I sat as near to him as I could without being obvious. There were two seats between us. Then, the usher came along and asked me to move over for late-comers, so I found myself sitting next to the black-haired young man.

The lecture was infuriating, and I scrawled many angry notes on my pocket pad. When it was over, the room was in an uproar, and I and the young man turned to each other to debrief. He introduced himself, then said he was there with his sister and her boyfriend. Would I like to meet them, come out for a drink?

Fate took my hand, and I said yes. For he was a relative of a famous Irish woman painter who had known Yeats and company, and the sister's boyfriend was a Nobel prizewinner, whose book on internment in the north of Ireland I had read. At the time, all that was secondary to David's compelling presence. It would be a difficult relationship. Most heavily karmic relationships are.

At the same time, I was struck by a girl in my Celtic mythology class. She had long blonde hair and a diffident manner. She was given to Oxford shirts and tweeds. Her name was Emily, and as much as I wanted to get to know her she avoided me. Then one day we discovered a mutual passion for Joyce and the Welsh language, and I was invited to her dormitory room for coffee. Her roommate, Dianna, was there, and when the conversation turned weird, Dianna did not depart. Emily and I soon found ourselves discussing hypnosis and past-life regression.

I confessed to having put someone under once, and—like Morey Bernstein and Bridey Murphy—we were on the way to a remarkable series of regressions.

Em and I went into the public study room, which was empty, closed the door and pulled the shade. Dianna had a test to study for so declined to join us, which was probably as well, as I don't think I could have handled everything coming out at once.

I was petrified. I didn't know if I could put her under on the one hand, or if I could get her out of it on the other. What if she uncovered something horrible and began to freak out? What if nothing happened? Swallowing all this, I led her down into a place of peaceful greyness, and back. Back through her childhood to the time before she was born. I then instructed her to go back to any time which had meaning for her now, and waited.

I really didn't expect anything to happen. I was floored when she answered my question as to where she found herself in a distinct and very authentic West of Ireland accent:

"Standing on a hill, looking at the sea."

"What are you doing there?"

"Waiting for Tom."

"Who's Tom?"

"Me beau."

"Does Tom have a last name?"

"Kilgallen." This clear and without hesitation. Kilgallen is a name specific to the area around Sligo town.

"What's your name?"

"Annie."

Annie went on to tell the tale that she and Tom, who cut turf for a living, were going to run away to Derry town because she was expecting a child. We moved onto Derry and she described her house, neighbourhood, and neighbours: Faolains, Sullivans, Learys next door. I felt an arctic blast of a chill. Ohmygod. I wanted to stop the dawning realization, but I knew the answer to my next question before I asked it:

"What are their names?"

"Paddy and Molly. They fight a lot. Always fighting. . ."

I wasn't listening much to her tale of the Learys' domestic woes, for I knew it viscerally; the alternating fights and intense sexuality, his IRA involvement, her artist lover who had been his student at Trinity College in Dublin. I knew too, who the dark-haired woman was, and why I was so compelled by David, why we fought so much. *This was the balance.*

Molly Leary, born Mary Margaret Clennaghan in Dublin in 1891, was the daughter of a prosperous Catholic banker from County Cavan and an Anglo-Irish socialite, whose father was stationed in Ireland in the (British) army. They were wealthy. She was a debutante before she met Patrick J. Leary, Lecturer in English at Trinity College and covert member of the Irish Republican Brotherhood (later the Irish Volunteers in 1916, and in 1920-1 the IRA). The lover mentioned above was a dark-haired man by the name of

Michael Rafferty from Rathbarren, County Sligo, and the brother of Anne Kilgallen.

But it got better, if you care for such melodrama, for not only was the young man in my mythology class (Kevin) my brother

William, who was killed at Ypres in October of 1914, but a fellow named Sullivan, the leader of our on-campus group, Students For A United Ireland, (soon to be Emily's beau) was Tom Kilgallen.

Lest you think I'm making this up for effect, that it's all too neat, let me point out that I did not know until I looked it up later that Kilgallen was specific to the area round Sligo Town. And I when I was in Ireland I came across a book, *The History of the IRA in Pictures; 1916 to the Present*, in which there was a photograph taken in 1921, during the Irish War for Independence, that was a dead ringer—excuse the pun—for Emily's beau. This man sat with an insolent grin for the camera, a Webley .45 casually pointed at the photographer. That qualifies for the far side of weird, in my book.

Later, Em's roommate wanted to see what would come up for her in a regression. She had had no part in what we were doing, knew nothing of it. I led her under and she began talking about her life as Kate Rafferty, a servant and nanny, in the house of a college professor and his wife in Dublin; her brother, Mick, who came to visit; and the funeral of "one of the rebels," and the oration given by a man named—and she called him this specifically—Padraig Pearse (rather than Patrick, as he is generally known), about whom she had nothing good to say.

I blanched at this last and stared over my pounding heart at Emily, whose hair was standing on end, and who was as bug-eyed as I. She gripped my leg so tightly she left marks, and I hushed her with a finger over my lips, though she had made no noise, and went on with the questions with as much neutrality as I could muster. We grilled Dianna later: Did she know who Padraig Pearse was, or Jeremiah O'Donovan Rossa? We were rewarded with a dismissive smirk. Of course she did not. She thought we had Ireland on the brain. And then we explained what she had said.

In August of 1915, Dublin saw the largest funeral cortege in the streets since the burial of the Irish Party leader Charles Stewart Parnell twenty-five years before; this one was for the ex-Fenian political prisoner Jeremiah O'Donovan Rossa, who had spent fifteen years in penal servitude in British prisons for his part in the bombings of Manchester in the 1870s. He endured the most degrading conditions and treatment, and was one of the few to live out his sentence and retain his sanity. He was a living hero to the Irish patriots, and when he died in New York his body was brought home to be interred with all honours in Dublin's Glasnevin Cemetery.

The man who gave the funeral oration was Padraig Pearse—Patrick to the world—poet, headmaster of a Gaelic school, leader of the Irish Volunteers who were at that moment in the final stages of preparation for the Uprising scheduled to take place on Easter Sunday, 1916. He used the funeral oration as a platform and an announcement of the Volunteers' intention. In 1916 he was the first President of the Irish Republic, the first signatory of the proclamation of such, the first to die when all the leaders were shot. William Butler Yeats wrote poems about him and revered his memory and what (mythologically) he stood for.

Dianna knew none of this. Kate Rafferty did.

Life got very weird. Em and Dianna and I spent a good deal of time unravelling the past; meanwhile, Emily and Sullivan and I pursued contemporary Irish politics.

I began working for Irish Northern Aid Committee, a rather more radical group than the Irish Forum, and joined naFianna Eireann, the (co-ed) Irish boy scouts (known to the unsympathetic as the junior IRA). I marched in protests, painted signs, publicly presented flowers to a survivor of 1916. It was my repayment to the good young men who gave their lives for their country, and the neighbours in Derry, for Molly hated them all because she hated her husband, and his dragging her to that depressing, nasty, *dirty* place. Karma, even self-karma, works that way: you become what you hate, so you understand it, have compassion for it, see that the person you hated is still a person, with the same need for love and happiness as you; and that the situation is a situation like any other. You get into it, and you do the best you can.

Kevin and I became friends, immersed in the mythology, and spent a lot of time together with the rest of the "Laurie Groupies," as we were called, in our lecturer's office discussing what was Real; that is to say, the unseen, how mythology explains, relates to, life.

David and I began falling apart, into the same old patterns we had engaged in before. Except that this time, I had better ammunition, and I knew when to get out.

There were some peculiar pieces of information that came up regarding Paddy's case, and its relation to David. Here are just a few:

Paddy's family had come to Dublin in 1897 from Muckross, near Killarney, County Kerry "because there was famine and rack-renting and we were starving."

He was a mad fan of Yeats', taught his work, and saw every play of his at the Abbey Theatre.

He likewise admired Maud Gonne and Constance Markievicz, friends of Yeats' and his own compatriots in rebellion.

In Dublin in 1986 I came upon the autobiography of Maud Gonne MacBride (Yeats' muse), in which she talks about working for the National Land League [the Fenians] in 1897 in Killarney *where there was rack-renting and the people were starving.*

David hated Dublin and anything to do with anything Irish, including Yeats. He had nothing good to say about the current political situation, and had been dragged, under protest, by his sister and her boyfriend to the meeting where we met. (A nice piece of role-reversal.)

His aunt, the artist, painted a portrait of Constance Markievicz (then Gore-Booth) and her sister outside their house in County Sligo.

David claimed he never could remember anything about the bad old days, but in one of our last rows before I left, he shouted at me: "Why are you blaming me for something I can hardly remember!" It was the "hardly" (which he later denied) I took to heart.

There were small validations along the way:

Molly called Paddy "Paidin" or "Padge," as his family did. I later discovered these nicknames are extremely common, though I had never heard them before. Not in *this* life, anyway!

David described to me once (late at night with a little help from John Barleycorn) the stretch of road from Baldoyle, County Dublin, to where Molly's parents' house stood, and what the house looked like, though he had never been there; and the scene at the Portmarnoc Races, where they met, which he had likewise never seen.

To end the cycle of karma between us, I did what Molly never had the courage to do: I left. That I left for Kevin, who then had been my brother, is only ironic and not really pertinent to the leaving. I knew it was what I had to do, should have done before, and did. It was Right Action. It was the herald of a whole new chapter of exploration.

Chapter Four

ॐ

Homeward Bound;
or, Tir na Nog

With our two-year-old, Kevin and I set off early in June of 1986 for the auld sod. I was going ostensibly to do my fieldwork, but as much to see old haunts again, and he was going because there were places he had missed seeing the last time around. We were not married, but our Irish travel agent assumed we were, and I was too shy to tell her we weren't; while Kevin thought it expedient amongst the Irish to let them assume we were, so we were booked as such at all our bed and breakfasts. I was not exactly happy about it—for it was rather like calling an ox a bull; he's grateful for the honour, but would rather have what's rightfully his—but I saw no point in making a fuss, even though I knew several Irish single parents; I had lived with two while I was pregnant.

Our journey was remarkably facilitated, and through a "fluke" our airfares were each cheaper than our son's. The universe expediting a necessary journey for me—and us. We came into Shannon at half-past seven of a clear lovely morning, and I knew this was to be overwhelming indeed. Coming down through the clouds, I caught my first sight in so many years (Molly died in 1928) of that green land, and burst into tears. Home. I was home again in Ireland. Land of my Mothers (for the Land of My Fathers [Welsh National Anthem] is Wales. My natural father is Welsh.) In Galway, Cork, and Tyrone, I have kin—separated now in the distance of time, but that never mattered to the Celts. Then there were the other descendants, Molly's and others. How would I fare, if I chanced upon one of them?

There were people sleeping on the plane. How could they sleep, coming home again to their native place, as if it were anywhere in the world? But, on looking around, I saw others peering down on the knowes and waterways of Shannonside with eyes as bright as mine. People of heart, likewise. I felt for the £20 note in my pocket. Time to use it at last! I had kept it for a month, exchanged from the bank downtown, tucked away. It made the journey seem real. And now it was real. I was home again in Ireland.

We went first to Quinn Abbey in County Clare, not far from our B&B, because of the early hour. On the way there, Kevin did not remember in which direction it lay, and when we came to a crossroads asked (expecting me to know), "Which way?" I saw a raven fly to the left.

"Left," says I. And there it was. Beautiful, haunting Quinn Abbey, standing in a field four miles off the Ennis road. Welcome to Ireland.

Once we were off the pavements, I knelt down and scooped up a handful of loamy earth beside the turnstile of the gate. My feet had not yet touched the soil proper, but I thought it beyond the beyonds, even for me, to kiss the ground. It was rich black earth, sticky and damp, and clumped together in my palm. I pocketed it (now an ossified lump in an earthenware bowl) and went into the Abbey behind Kevin and Rudraigh.

Inside was the gravestone of the last local chieftain, Sean Buide MacNamara, patriot of the uprising of 1798. Kevin was off looking at something else, so I stood a moment and gave the Chieftain my honours, promising that he and his comrades would not be forgotten. Then, quite without my volition, I raised my arm in a salute above my head. It just seemed like the right thing to do, but, once it was raised, I stared at it as if it belonged to someone else, or had a mind of its own, horrified for the resonances of the Nazis. Then the recollections rose up: Ireland under Brian Boru, Viking Norway, Iron Age Scotland, Rome, Greece, Macedonia, Egypt. And my horror abated. The Nazis corrupted that salute for the world (as they did the symbol of the sun god, the swastika) but it was *the* mark of respect in the ancient world amongst warriors.

And the evening and the morning were the first day.

In Killinaboy, a tiny village outside Corofin in the County Clare, stood my midwife Lelia Larkin's house. And up on the hill was the ruined church which was ruined even in the 17th century, for Cromwell's troops had laid it waste. Above the door I remembered there being a sheila-na-gig—an old fertility carving—and there she was with her fierce face, displaying all her womanly charms to the world. As I stood there, trying to think of a way to reach her, for it was good luck to rub her belly, I could hear the voice of Lelia's aunt and teacher, Moira, saying, "And see you that over there, girl, there's whitethorn. Will you tell me now what it is good for?"

I looked up, half-expecting to see her tall rangy figure with its mass of silvered black hair hanging down. I smiled a little as I found an old plastic flower bucket to climb on, and I was Lelia again, broad of beam, reaching up to honour the sheila, hoping it would bring her and her Johnny a child.

At Lemanagh castle ruins, I saw the well-remembered home of our landlady, Maire Rua O'Brien, to whom John had gone to ask for our parcel of land. She was not a handsome woman, our red-haired Mary, as pictures of her at the Clare Heritage Centre in Corofin bore out.

In Ennis Town, I stood on the very spot on the pavements where John Larkin was killed, and his ghost cried out to me, as it had done when Lelia waited on the road. The scene was before my eyes: John with his woolly dark hair hanging down from under his black caubeen, his gentle eyes gone steely and cold. They would not move him this time, for he had been put out on the roads once by Cromwell's soldiers. He stood his ground, and he died in blood in the public street before he could be removed to a house or tavern, his only thought that Lelia had been right, and now he was leaving her alone. He should have listened. . .

The past was so clear and easily reached here! Though the place was old, even in towns there were not layers of modernity to cut through. It was heavenly sweet.

One of the hazards of being organically weird is that you can never be sure if someone you're meeting is "real" or not. In one case, the encounter was doubly strange.

At Yeats' Tower, Thoor Ballylee, in County Galway, we came back down to our car to see a tall old man in salt-and-pepper tweeds suddenly appear from nowhere in the parking lot. His feet made no noise on the gravel. He came directly to us and began chatting us up. He asked us if we had been to a stone fort nearby in the Burren (we had), and told us a story of one of his visits there:

It was a misty morning, not unlike the one that day, and he had hiked up from the road (seven miles). Sitting there in the middle of the fort, appearing through the mist, was a man with long red hair and an equally long red beard. Thinking him one of the Faery Folk, he uncertainly hailed the fellow, whereupon the wee one—for he was a little wiry man, hardly as tall as I, I was told—leapt up in great fright and let out a shriek.

"Where did you come from?" demanded the red-haired man.

"From the path," replied our tweedy friend, pointing back the way he'd come.

The redheaded man gaped at him. "There's a *road?*"

Our friend frowned. "Of course. . .." He began to get a peculiar feeling and asked, "How did you get here?"

The redheaded man pointed out into the plain. "D'ye see that village?" It was about twenty miles away.

"Aye," said our friend.

"I walked from there, and climbed up the cliff, so. [Which was a good two-hundred feet high.] I didn't know there was another way up here."

I point out that the fort was heavily occupied in the Iron Age, up until the Christian period. The redheaded man wore very non-descript, "anytime" clothes—dark trousers and a loose jacket.

After telling this story, our tweedy friend smiled benignly, and said, "What do you think of that?" Then he bid us good day—made a bow—and turned and walked away, literally disappearing into thin air.

How many layers of reality were operating there? For our tweedy friend could easily have been some local gentryman in the previous century. You can never tell, especially in Celtia!

Onward up the west coast we went, staying in the Gaelic-speaking area of Connemara. We were making a deosil (clockwise) circuit around the country, according to the old custom. As we came into County Sligo—home of W.B. Yeats, and of Molly's artist—I looked out at the mountains to the west. I was seeking *his* mountains, Mick's home place. We passed the village of Collooney on our way up to Sligo Town, and I felt a wash of recognition. *Those are his mountains.* Molly had been to Sligo only once, visiting Mick's old father. But I knew the place, from his talk, from his paintings.

At our B&B, at the foot of Ben Bulben, I enquired of the landlady Anne Hennigan—who with her flock of children and blonde colouring brought Anne Kilgallen rushing to mind—how to get to Rathbarren.

"Rat'buurn?" she asked in the soft Sligo burr. I stared up at her, for she said it exactly in the manner Mick had done. "Sure, there's only one place I know of by that name. There's a Protestant church there."

She gave me the directions: follow the road to Ballisodare, and when you come to Collooney crossroads, turn and take the road up under the railroad bridge. It's about a mile to Coolaney. Enquire at the pub from there.

So I did, and was met with a very tall old man with a shock of long white hair. He gave me a shock, for he was the image of Mick's father. His name was even Sean! He brightened on hearing I was looking for Rathbarren, and happily gave me directions, saying,

"Go up the road a pace to the end of the village and past the railroad station—sure, the train used to stop here, but it hasn't for years gone—and you'll see the spire through the trees, so."

The train used to stop here. The train from Derry.

And the long journey bringing Anne's body home to rest in its native soil, with her flock of children round—for they had never seen their grandfather—when Molly was so ill of TB. That hideous journey. Lonely and tired and sick, missing Mick, who was gone to America. *It was all real. It really happened here.*

I looked on the scene of Collooney with an eye for the bright young man who had sketched it as a child, who had gone to Dublin to university by the bequest of his landlord, Charles Keane. Such was my memory. Such I had written, for it was my design to turn the story of that life into a novel. The name of the landlord was entirely unverified by outside sources.

A few days later we were at Glencolumbcille in Donegal, and in a shop there I found a book on progressive Irish landlords of the 19th century. I opened it up at random, and there was an entry about Charles Keane O'Hara—the O'Hara of Leyney—of Annaghmore, near Rathbarren, County Sligo, who was not only a progressive farmer, but a noted philanthropist. Kevin says of my exclamations at such occurrences: "Why are you continually surprised? This happens to you all the time." I am because there is always margin for error, because I have been encultured—like everyone else—to doubt.

Verifying Mick's existence, Mick's story, was not the only weird part of our time in Sligo. The day we arrived, before we even went to Mrs. Hennigan's farm at the foot of Ben Bulben, we stopped at Carrowmore, a cairn not far from Lough Gill (and the Lake Isle Of Innisfree, for Yeats fans). We got out of our little red Austin and hiked over to the field in which the cairn stood. There, standing sentinel, was a large black bullock. It was the Tain Bo Cuailligne (the Cattle Raid of Cooley, or The Book of the Dun Cow, one of the earliest surviving pictures of pre-Christian Ireland) sprung to life. There was no way he was going to let us into *his* field, or near *his* cairn.

With extreme caution we edged into the field, while the bull kept a weather eye on us all the while. We must have circled the cairn at least three times (and I do not remember if it was deosil or widdershins, but plainly it was Their object that we circle it) before Angus Og—for so I called him, after the Iron Age hero—came charging. Scooping up the child, I made a mad leap for the safety of the outer circle of the cairn, where the bullock could not advance. I was trepidaceous about entering the inner sanctum of the cairn, where the remains had once been laid. (For this one was without its covering of stones and earth.) I asked, "Is it safe?" not so much to Kevin as to Them.

Kevin replied, "Oh sure, we did it last time."

Wary, I stepped over the threshold of the inner part of the cairn, and like Arianrhod in the Welsh myth Mabinogi, a gush of water came—not from me, not from imminent labour, but from the skies. Sudden rain came pelting, blinding. So much for listening to those who don't know Them! We were soaked to the skin in a moment. This continued until, with great caution, we made our way out of the far side of the cairn and over the stone fence. We made our wide circuit thus out of the reach of Angus Og, and back to the car.

The rain diminished to faint sprinkles. By the time we were back down to the Sligo road, a bare quarter-mile away, it became clear that it had not rained there. When we arrived at Mrs. Hennigan's, she commented on our sodden state.

"We were caught in the rain a few minutes ago," I told her.

She looked at me queerly. "It didn't rain today," she said.

We tried very hard in the next two days to get to Knocknarea, which is known locally (erroneously, according to one local scholar) as Maeve's Cairn. It was Maeve who was responsible for the Tain Bo Cuailligne, wanting all things to be equal betwixt herself and her husband Ailill (the Celts having a very progressive society where women were concerned). It was Maeve with whom I had been associated in Kevin's and everybody else's mind: the woman warrior. And indeed, I have a great fondness for her. Her alleged cairn is enormous, a small mountain, and sits out in the middle of a field near Rosses' Point. It is impossible to miss, and easy to get to, especially with Ordinance Survey maps.

We tried every marked and unmarked road on the land for two days, but could not gain access to the sacred place. We wound round in circles, as we had done at Imbolc in Northern California. It is a rule in Celtic countries: if you're meant to be there, you'll get there; if you're not, there is no force under heaven that'll get you there. Not if They don't want you to be there. And for some reason, They did not want me there (Kevin had climbed on top of it on his last visit).

Perhaps they knew I would be called away to Faery by their music, and that I had work to do. In any case, we were reduced to viewing the crystalline cairn sparkling in the mocking sun from afar, and take comfort in the words of our scholar friend that it belonged not to Maeve at all, but a chieftain buried there in the 1100s. Sour grapes, maybe, and maybe Michael Quirk was right, but it was a further illustration—as if I or we needed any, of the power of the Other-world. You don't mess with Them, puny human.

At the Grianan of Ailech, on the border of Counties Donegal and Derry, I had my first experience in almost seventy years of the wind that blew continually off Lough Foyle (at the head of which sits Derry town). I had written in *Dark Rosaleen*, Molly's story, of her first view of the town the morning after her arrival:

> *stinking air, billowing grey clumps of smoke over grey row houses, Derry stood on the River Foyle like an oozing scab on a sore. . .It was the shrill of factory horns that awakened her from her few hours of light sleep. . .[she] flew to the window to see only women and girls hurrying toward their factories in the grey morning light, shawls flung over their heads and clutched or pinned at the throat. . .The Bogside, the ancient home of the dispossessed natives. . .Their own street was on such a steep hill that the best exercise one could get would be a walk to the corner. . .there was not green land in sight beyond that bog, and the cold and windy lake, whose wind was ceaseless.*

Of Derry I remembered most the dreary grey, almost continually rainy weather, that ceaseless cold wind, our steep street, and the murderous Black and Tans, who were every bit as vile as the various Unionist factions of the 1980s. Standing beside the ancient stone house of the Grianan on the hill overlooking Lough Foyle, I felt that bitter wind again. And bitter were the memories it brought with it. Every bit of the history I remembered from the 1920s was borne out in later minute research, up to and including the raid upon the Catholic Bogside in 1920 by the Tans. If I had any doubts, they were there dispelled.

There is a Derryman, Phil Coulter, whose much-beloved song, "The Town I Loved So Well," verified my memories down to minutiae. Derry people (and I) love it, for it lauds their courage and their great heart:

In my memory I will always see
The town that I have loved so well
. . .In the early morning the shirt-factory horns
called women from Creggan, the Moor and the Bog
. . .though their spirit's been bruised, never broken
still they'll not forget, for their hearts are set
on tomorrow and peace once again

I wanted very much to go to the Bogside, as much to stand in our old street—to look out across the plain as I did every morning then, to feel the wind, and the cobbles beneath my feet—as to stand at Free Derry Corner at the entrance to the Bogside (called so because the butt end of the house is painted, in great red letters, "You Are Now Entering Free Derry") where in 1967 Bernadette Devlin and the rest of the peaceful protesters were fired upon by the British army, thus heralding the latest segment of The Troubles. (Until that time the British Army would not enter the Bogside.) I had met Bernie in San Francisco and admire her greatly.

But Kevin would have none of it, refused even to let me rent a bicycle and cycle from Letterkenny in Donegal (about twenty-five miles), as I offered to do. His excuse was that we had to be in Dundalk, across the country, next day. Bad enough we had to drive across the North at all, in his opinion (but there were Neolithic, Bronze, and Iron Age sites there he wanted to see).

I was not afraid of the North. What I had endured before had inured me to fear of anything it currently had to offer in the way of bombings or commandeering of cars. Besides, we were American tourists in a car with number plates from the Free State. We would not be troubled. But he would have none of it. It caused quite a row. I thought he was a coward, and he thought I was selfish and reckless. It was in this frame of mind, of mutual antipathy, that we traveled to Dublin, where the reality of the past would be undeniably confronted.

We came down the east coast from Dundalk, and our first stop before "Dear Dirty Dublin" was Baldoyle, about twelve miles north of the capitol. This was where Molly (and her brother Liam—Kevin) had grown up. I had my own memories of the house's situation, had made a painting of it, and had directions to it from my guides. Our directions were from the "end of town," and I was determined to follow them precisely, even though when we came down we passed the road on the right, and I felt a chill of recognition. *That's It!*

The directions were to travel "N on the main road, about a mile [it was ¼], turn on the road that comes on the left, go another mile, turn up the road on the right, go up the lane that comes up on the immediate left, keep going and there you are."

And there we were, with horses in the paddock and all (Liam and Molly raised horses as a lucrative avocation) exactly as I had described it, written about it: A late "Queen Anne" Victorian brick house, with a yellow door and white "fancywork" on the eaves.

I went up to the door to ask if I could take pictures and a very old woman with great big hazel eyes and an upper-class accent answered the door. As I wrote in my journal, "I have the terrible fear it was Sally [Molly's oldest daughter]." I looked in at the front windows, and to the right was the breakfast room, to the left the front parlour, with the same Regency mirror and Empire Revival furniture in the very same places I recalled (which Molly's mother would not allow any to sit on). At a gate nearby there was a great garden, and behind that, a tennis court. Around to the right were the outbuildings, stables and such.

My house. Home. That room right up there in the back, overlooking the stable yard, was mine. Some things had changed—there was a solarium—but it was my house. And my daughter, now an old woman. How like her father she looked, with those great hazel eyes! And I thought, Paddy Leary is rolling in his grave to see his cherished cailin rua (red-haired girl), his Sally, living in the house of the people he hated so, his wife's people; the gentry.

I was elated, jumping up and down like a child in the rain, running all about gleefully snapping pictures left right and centre, for the old woman had not gainsaid me, only asked, "How did you find us?"— not "Who are you, you crazy Yank, and what do you want?" but "How did you find us?" That in itself was a genuine miracle. Meanwhile, in the car Kevin was squirming. He didn't like the whole resonance of that life, and here was undeniable proof that what I said was true. I could feel him looking at me the entire time I capered about, wishing me to have done already, but for once I was determined to be selfish indeed. It was the only time in this life I would be here, and I wanted to savour it.

When the film was gone, I clambered back into the car in my muddy knee-boots to hear his muttered, "Let's get out of here," as he drove very quickly down the driveway and back toward Dublin. But I didn't care if he was discomfited, for I had found my house. I waved a gay farewell to the thoroughbreds in the paddock as we sailed past, happy as I had never been before in my life.

Onward to Dublin. One of my Irish friends had recommended

Nancy Flynn's, a B&B, "coincidentally," in Gardiner Street, which happened to be the street Paddy and Molly lived in, and Nancy Flynn's was a bare half-block from Leary's at Number 60 Mountjoy Square. That Nancy Flynn was also sympathetic to The Cause was icing on the cake.

We passed the house as we went up Gardiner Street from the quayside. There it was, across from the park, third from the corner; white door, lovely glasswork fanlight. Three floors and servants' quarters above that, with the kitchens below. A typical Georgian townhouse, such as viewers of *Upstairs Downstairs* would recognize. We settled in at Nancy's, and then I went racing down the block to take pictures, pausing in dismay before the front door.

What had they done to it, my lovely house! Above the second floor all the windows were boarded up. I went round the back, and the garden was a sight, with weeds as tall as I. And when I came back to the front of the house, the people who lived there were taking a motorcycle (!!!!!) out of the front hallway. My lovely chandelier was all tarnished and broken; the chandelier of Cavan Glass that was a wedding present from my father. I thought that Paddy would be furious to see to what use his study was being put [a studio apartment]. *I* was furious. My poor lovely house. It was ironic indeed that my house in Clare from the 17th century was in better shape than my Dublin one from the 20th.

Across the street from Nancy Flynn's was St. Francis Xavier's Catholic Church—the church I remembered from my fainting episode four years before; Francis Xavier's, extolled by Joyce in *Portrait of the Artist as a Young Man*. I went inside, and there was a Mass going on. I lurked at the back like a furtive Protestant, full of all the old bad feelings, for Molly had been a Catholic by default and attended Mass only reluctantly as a public duty. Then too, there was the memory of the fainting day, 1912. She had lost her child that day. The memory was too painful. I put a coin in the box for the preservation of the church (which was badly wanting repairs, according to the placard) and left. I did attend Mass on the Sunday morning following, but it too was joyless.

In the four days we spent in Dublin, I visited the site of Mick Rafferty's house in Townsend street (a photograph of which—exactly as I had written of it, sketched it—I later found in a book on The Troubles; the photo was taken during the Easter Rising, 1916); Paddy's bachelor quarters in Anne street, adjacent to the University; and Bewley's Cafe in D'Olier street, where Mick and Molly used to meet. I went in search of a painting of Mick's—of Molly as An

Roisin Dubh, The Dark Rosaleen, Ireland—which I did not find. And chanced upon his reincarnation one evening as we went strolling in O'Connell Street, even as Dubs have done for at least three hundred years of summer evenings when the light holds sway until nearly midnight.

For nearly two years I had had an astral friendship with this young man, who came to me one night in a dream, confused by images he had of a ghastly death in a Dublin house. (Mick had gassed himself in Townsend Street after Molly died.) I was his teacher in esoteric matters, his friend, and he had told me before my coming to Ireland to look for him in Dublin. He would not tell me where. But knowing he was a labourer, I expected it to be in that capacity. I knew his face, and finally, as we were walking across the river to the Coombe to visit a friend of mine, I saw him.

It was in O'Connell street, the main street in town, between the news-agents' where Paddy had been thunked on the head by the Dublin Metropolitan Police in the Bloody Sunday riots in 1913, and the General Post Office, where Patrick Pearse and company had proclaimed the Irish Republic in 1916. I heard the command "*look up!*" as we passed some scaffolding and there he was, smiling down at me, curly black hair, green eyes and all, paintbrush in hand as he worked on the trim of the building. Michael Kilbride.

Some may think this was just some boyo smiling at a pretty girl, but this pretty girl had a man and a toddler in tow. Hardly an advert for availability. And when our eyes met, it was electric. It was he and no other. He who had been, among others, to me John Larkin and Bathurst Skelton—Martha Jefferson's first husband. Dear Michael. My "little brother." When I looked back, he was still looking on, and I realized that he was paint-covered, weary; that he had a companion with him. I had missed all that on first glance, for the intensity of the meeting.

I never saw him again. We talked, as we had done for two years; but not long after my return to the States, I tuned in for our weekly chat and he sounded awfully funny. His "speech" was slow and distorted, as one suffering from stroke, and I knew immediately that something terrible had happened.

—*Michael! What's the matter with you?*
—*I have been killed.*
—*WHAT HAPPENED?!* His girlfriend was newly pregnant, and they were going to get married.
—*I was coming off the An Lar (City Centre) bus, and*

stepped out to cross the road, and didn't see the lorry that was passing.

So that gentle, hard-working young man's life came to an end. He was nineteen years old. Nineteen years which he had given up by offing himself in 1933. The shock I felt on the suddenness was, on reflection, replaced by a peaceful sense that he had fulfilled his mission and incorporated all he'd come to do. Such is death when you've seen the Other side. As D.H. Lawrence would have it, "only old tired men taking off their shirts."

But death was much on my mind when we were in Dublin, for we had a terrific electrical storm which made sleep impossible, both for the noise and the memories it evoked of Easter Week, 1916, and the Uprising. I kept vigilant all night and into the morning while Kevin and Rudraigh slept, watching the storm, listening to the crash of thunder, remembering those awful times.

Molly went to the races on Easter Monday—as did everyone in Dublin who could afford the tramfare—taking her children, as they were supposed to go to her parents' in Baldoyle afterward, but leaving Paddy behind, who begged off because he supposedly had to fetch something from the university. "Be along, love, I'll catch you up later." He did not, of course, being one of the rebels. He joined in the fray, fighting with the Yank, DeValera, at Jacob's biscuit factory. At the end of Easter Week, when the surrender had come, he rode out to Baldoyle on a bicycle he stole from somewhere, more dead than alive from hunger, exhaustion, and grief. His dream of a free Ireland lay in ruins.

During Easter Week, the British bombed and burnt the town (O'Connell Street lay in ruins for half its length afterward), and in Baldoyle we climbed up on the roof to watch Dublin in flames and hear the crash of the shells over the city and the gossip brought home by my father from the village: the rebels had sacked the city, and so forth (the newspapers and telephones were all shut down, so we had no news except gossip). And Molly was left to wonder about the safety of her house, her friends, her husband. As little as she cared for him, she had no desire to be left a widow.

All this the storm brought back to me again vividly. I have always hated thunderstorms, for they remind me of war and death, but no more hateful did I find them than then, looking out the window in that long night in my old neighbourhood.

Most of my Molly-jaunts were accomplished in "mere" sightseeing around the town, with Kevin and Rudraigh. Trinity College and environs had other lures besides the personal past. But there was one jaunt I accomplished alone, and that was a meeting with the publicity director of Sinn Fein in Parnell Square. Alone I went, and alone I had a chat and tea with engaging Brian about the current political situation. I invited Kevin, but he wanted no part of it, even though I assured him that it would be no more dangerous than a chat with my friend Mairead in the Coombe, and that Brian was a nice friendly fellow even though he admitted to liking Nancy Flynn, and indeed most of my rebelly friends. I think the resonances were too much for him. And he believed the danger-tales, the like of which Tom Clancy's *Patriot Games* were made. I laughed at their complete absurdity, knowing things as I did from the inside.

We were trailed by G-men as we went window-shopping one afternoon, but what harm could they do us, little family? All we had to do was present our perfectly authentic American passports—with the implication of perfectly authentic pots of American money to go with them—and there would be an end to it. This security was the cause of all my gaiety. They couldn't hurt me now. Not me, nor any of my kin. The bad old days were over.

Kevin says himself that he was a right bastard when we were in Dublin, and so he was: withdrawn, surly, niggardly of soul. I can hardly blame him, for his entire reality base was being challenged, and I'm sure my blethering on about the memories that poured forth didn't help. But I had to tell someone, and he *had* been there. Like as not, he was sick to death of the whole subject and wanted to throttle me.

He has since complained that there were times he didn't know who I was—that *I* didn't know who I was; but I was always firmly in grip of my identity; I might say "I" when talking about Molly—or anyone else—as the memories come first-person, but I have never lost my sense of being in two places at once, being Kelly watching the drama of the past, however acutely I might feel the emotions the memories evoke. It is a basic misunderstanding of beingness which I'm not certain can be wholly breached. Intellectually, because I tell him, Kevin can understand my experience of reality, but until he's experienced it himself, he never will really understand, in his soul. It is describing a blind man to an elephant: you have to trust that the elephant gets it, for he can't articulate and you don't speak elephant.

To round out the Molly-life resonances in Ireland, when we were in County Kerry, where Paddy Leary was from, I came to terms with Paddy there, and forgave him, and David. Standing in the field where his family's farm had been, I understood him better than Molly had done when she was there on their honeymoon, for I felt the land in the same way that Paddy did. The high black mountains and musical jangling of the Kerry accent spoke to my soul as they did to Paidin's and I allowed myself there to remember his good qualities and the happy times. I forgave him (and David) for being a rotten bastard, and went home to write his part of the story in utter sympathy to him, in a balanced and thoughtful way.

The journey to Ireland had healed those old wounds, left gaping for sixty-odd years, and for such it was a rousing success. I had accomplished my fieldwork, visited dear friends, made new ones. It was only my relationship with Kevin that had shown its inadequacies, fallen apart. It's said that traveling with someone will do that.

As a grace note, when we were in Kinsale, County Cork, where some of my Irish ancestors came from, I met with Herself—Eiriu, Ireland—one night as I sat down by Harbour Hill watching the sunset (at half-past eleven P.M.). She appeared across the waters of the harbour like Miss Woodruff in *The French Lieutenant's Woman*, a mournful figure in a dark-grey cloak; or like Maud Gonne in Yeats' *Countess Cathleen*: tall, gaunt, hollow-eyed. She hovered above the waters at the edge of the harbour, not far from me and spoke in a grave and commanding voice:

> *You are of this place. You are my servant. You have seen the land and the people, and know their joys and grief. They are my joys, my grief. Much time have you spent on these shores, from the time of the Milesians. My people are your people; their soul will never leave you. You may leave this place, but it will never leave you. You will return to us one day.*

This last was not an invitation or a prophecy, but a command, to which I promised that I would return. Meanwhile, I had a book to finish, Molly's story, in which she too had been compared to Ireland by Mick in his painting and Paddy in his bright dreams of freedom. I was moved by my experiences and my encounter with Herself to end the story with a poem, *The Rebel*, by Patrick Pearse:

> *I am flesh of the flesh of these lowly*
> *I am bone of their bone*
> *I that have never submitted;*
> *I that have a soul greater than the soul of my people's*
> *masters,*

I that have vision and prophecy and the gift of fiery speech,
I that have spoken with God on the top of his holy hill.
And because I am of the people, I understand the people,
I am sorrowful with their sorrow, I am hungry with their desire:
My heart has been heavy with the grief of mothers
My eyes have been wet with the tears of children,
I have yearned with old wistful men
And laughed or cursed with young men. . .
. . .And now I speak, being full of vision. . .

Chapter Five

ॐ

All Together Now;
or, The Gang's All Here

I have spoken of my guides, the Guys Upstairs, the Gang in the Green Room, and more specifically of Irene, who is my personal contact—the voice of the group to me—my guardian angel if you will. How I came to know her features in my unravelling of Molly/Mick/Paddy, and, in itself, launched an entire area of exploration of doorways of time and the nature of the true reality.

I had flirted with a Ouija board off and on and decided well before my Irish journey to see what would come up about all that jazz in the 1890s-1920s. What I got was the personality of Molly Leary and her viewpoint. Intrigued, I decided to see if I could do the same with the others, if their viewpoints of particular incidences would be any different. And were they ever! I learned, blushing through many a session with Paddy Leary, that the resonance of personality definitely lingers on the Akashic Plane, and in the Record! He was as rude and blunt as he had ever been in life. He had not changed. But, I thought, what should one expect from a Leo with an Aries rising?

What I was contacting is the part of his soul that would forever hold the memory and personality of that lifetime. He was as much Patrick Leary as my friend David, or any other personality he had been. So was I, so are we all. I personally believe this is why ghosts exist, even though their souls move on, because the patterning of an essence is indelibly writ on the place and time in which the personality lived, as well as in the ethers.

I talked with all the old crew from Ireland: Molly, Mick, Paddy, Anne, Tom, Katie, even the children. Finally, I began to see that no one had an objective picture of the incidents, but all their own little pieces of the puzzle, so I asked my guides what had "really" happened. What had objectively occurred in the historical, factual, agreed-upon time-space consensus reality. And it was in some cases exactly matching so-and-so's recollection, and in some cases wildly varying. But it *all* "happened." Moral: never call anyone a liar or question his reality. How do you know but it's "more real," more valid, than yours?

During the course of this objective research, I got tired of calling on Them as "my spirit guides." It felt corny and rather childish. So I asked one day what I could call them instead, and they answered:

> *In one of the last lifetimes of one of us, we were known as Irene. This personality "died" in the 13th century. You may call us this if you wish, but one name-label is as valid as any other. You may as well call us Mickey Mouse or Henry VIII, although that personality was not part of our little group.*

That is how I met Irene. Her last lifetime had been as a nun in France in the 13th century, in Lorraine, and if a 13th-century French nun sounds familiar, it's because Cathleen and Irene and Cathleen's guide Charmaigne were all at the same nunnery. I myself was a monk and knew them only on the astral then, but we swapped experiences—war stories—in dream-time, for we are, vibrationally speaking, Warriors all. (More on that in a moment.) "Physically"—if there is a need to manifest a visual image at all—Irene looks like nothing more than Joan of Arc: a fairly small, stocky person of a "female" resonance, wearing chain mail and a tabard. "Her" teeth aren't very good, but "she's" a handsome person nonetheless. Very down-to-earth. A rustic sense of humour. Fond of teasing, irony, and puns as They all are.

This was the introduction of another piece of the puzzle. Kevin came back from a trip to our favourite bookshop with a paperback by a favourite author of his. He thought I would find it interesting, validating, and helpful. I don't think he expected it to quite unlock the whole universe as it did. Maybe if he had he'd have left it in the shop. Maybe it was inevitable. *I* felt like Helen Keller, standing at the pump with Miss Sullivan finger-spelling w-a-t-e-r into her outstretched hand: "wah-wah." The light dawned, the connection was made, and mourning became electra. My whole soul said *YES* to the information in a way unprecedented and unmatched since.

The book was a non-fiction work called *Messages From Michael*, published by PEI Books (Playboy Paperbacks) in 1980, about a group of people in Berkeley who had been channeling an entity named Michael on the Ouija board for about seventeen years. The author—editor—was Chelsea Quinn Yarbro, whose St. Germaine novels—about a vampire who travels through time—Kevin admired so much. This book—and the others which followed—spawned a group and a System of Explaining The Nature of Reality (*not* a religion) known as the Michael Teaching. It is similar to the later channeled information from Seth, via Jane Roberts.

The basic reality is that we are all a part of All That Is—which Michael calls the Tao, as it has fewer gender-specific connotations in our Western society than "God"—and this Oneness is timeless, ever cycling round and round: souls (fragments) being cast from it to go play in the universe; coalescing into larger groups (entities) who spend their "time" on the physical plane together, until they're sufficiently detached from the fascination of it; whereupon they join back together as one and expand increasingly with other groups until they are absorbed once more into All That Is and the whole thing starts over again, *ad infinitum*. With me so far?

As with refractions of light, souls (fragments) have seven possible basic vibrational frequencies, one of which is chosen for a particular whole cycle (from casting to reunification with All That Is). These vibrational frequencies are known as *Roles in Essence* and are:

On the Inspiration Axis:
Priests, who serve the Higher Good, whatever they perceive that to be.
Servers (used to be Slaves before the term became Politically Incorrect), who serve the Common Good, whatever they perceive that to be.

On the Expression Axis:
Artisans, whose urge is to create (beauty, reality) in a material way.
Sages, whose urge is to create with words, concepts.

On the Action Axis:
Kings, who command the forces, lead by example.
Warriors, who follow the flags, require a challenge.

And in the Neutral Position:
Scholars, who have access to all the above, but whose basic urge is to observe, integrate.

Roles in Essence have nothing to do with one's job in life, although, obviously, Warriors are very comfortable being soldiers, and Priests being, well Priests. But Queen Victoria, for example, was a Server, so you can't get too hung up on labels. Terms are (as I am frequently reminded by Them) merely convenient tags for concepts, expressions of beingness. Michael says it is possible for all Roles to experience all of life in the cycle, courtesy of the overleaves (personality traits) which change each lifetime. The Role in Essence does not change. Once you choose it, you're stuck with it until about the mid-Causal Plane.

The other overleaves are *Age, Level, Goal, Mode, Attitude, Centering* (and Part of Centering), and everyone's favourite—*Chief Feature* (a sort of Achilles Heel we all choose each time as a challenge; there are no good Chief Features).

The Ages of the soul are: Infant, Baby, Young, Mature, Old, and (off the physical plane) Transcendental, and Infinite. (After that everybody's All One Together, so what's the point of Age?)

Within each of the ages are seven levels. ["Kittens, cats, sacks, wives, how many were going to St. Ives?" It's really not as complex as it seems at first. Just think to yourself that the universe is founded on Base Seven, and you'll be home free.]

The Goals are: Growth, Retardation, Acceptance, Rejection, Dominance, Submission, and Stagnation.

The Modes are: Passion, Repression, Power, Caution, Aggression, Perseverance, and Observation.

The Attitudes are: Spiritualist, Stoic, Idealist, Skeptic, Realist, Cynic, and Pragmatist.

The Centers are: Higher Emotional, Emotional, Higher Intellectual, Intellectual, Higher Moving, Moving, Sexual, and Instinctive. Nobody is permanently centred in the Higher Centres, not even Jesus Christ, Mohammed, Gandhi, Lao Tzu, or the Buddha. Though they were there more than most of us.

The Chief Features are: Arrogance, Self-Deprecation, Greed (fixated on something), Self-Destruction, Impatience, Martyrdom, and Stubbornness. Most people have one main CF and a secondary. Really old souls—those on their last lifetimes, or those off the physical plane, don't have to have CFs, but they're the only ones.

My own overleaves this time (to let it all hang out) are: Sixth-Level Old Warrior, a Spiritualist in the Passion Mode, in the Intellectual Part of the Emotional Centre, with a Goal of Acceptance, and a Primary Chief Feature of Self-Deprecation and a Secondary of Impatience.

All of which means my primary beingness is to act; I'm real old; I'm nearly done; I react strongly to things; I think about God (or the Nature of Beingness) a lot; I ponder why I feel the way I do (and where it resonates from); I want to let people do their things (and want them to let me do my thing too); I fear I haven't done it right, or fast enough.

The basic Michael Teaching, in a nutshell. Sorry folks, that's about as simple as it gets.

But once you understand the basic information, the way personalities work (or don't work) together, it can be applied to every situation, to every lifetime, and can serve as a basis for understanding between two souls (fragments). Which is, after all what we're here for. All these overleaves are chosen by the soul before a particular lifetime to facilitate the lessons, karma, agreements, and so forth of that lifetime. There is no one "up there" telling you what you have to be. All Is Choice. (Basic Choice Lecture. The variations number in the hundreds of thousands. Ask Kevin, Cathleen, Wendy, or anyone else we've turned on to this teaching.)

And a turning on is what this has become: a broad-based, Oh-you-have-to-read-this-book club. There is no dogma in it. It fits with any religion or viewpoint. (If you're open-minded. You do rather have to accept that there are more things in heaven and earth than are met with in your philosophy.) We (those of us enumerated above) have given the book to literally scores of friends, who in turn have given it to others, so the effect just from us has been in the hundreds of people.

There was one college friend I gave it to, however, an older woman, who shrugged at it dismissively. "Oh yeah," she said, "I read that." I was aghast. *And it hadn't changed her life?!* I thought she must not have read it very carefully.

Then there are the full circles: recently, Wendy gave a copy to her father (who had welcomed me into the Catholic Church), as he is undergoing a personal and spiritual transition, and it has helped him, brought him a tremendous sense of peace. Instant good karma for John, for having facilitated me all those years ago.

Having explained life, the universe, and everything according to Michael, I will now say that it is no more or less valid, useful, etc., than any other means of explaining the universe, whether numerology, tarot, astrology, or orthodox (or unorthodox) religion. It is succinct, and undogmatic, but its primary usefulness is that it gave Kevin and me a common ground, a common language, and in its more in-depth teaching validated what I (and we all) knew about the way the universe works. It opened things up. (Thanks, Kev. You did good.)

Now that I had the keys, I could unlock all the doors as fast as I chose and see what prizes lay behind them. The treasures were rich and rare and very old.

Before our Irish sojourn, I went to a fellow mystic to unravel some knotty problems from Mick and Molly, and when we had done with that, she asked me to go back to the first time we were together. I don't think she was prepared for my answer! For I described to her being an amorphous being of light, very close to, yet separate from All That Is (casting!) and my grief at becoming a separate amorphous being of light from my dear one. Dori told me to go forward in time a few million years, and we came to something recognizable as a proto-human existence.

One of the lifetimes we explored which had nothing to do with Mick, which "merely" had "resonance for me in this lifetime" was one as a hermit in the Tibetan Himalayas in the middle of the 15th century. I saw the body clearly: long black hair, white clothes, long nails, a man of peace, who had been a physician in his former occupation as a monk. He sat cross-legged in a tiny stone cell with one window, overlooking the grey-white of the holy mountains. "Raji," I came to call him.

This was a title, not a name, for his name in Tibetan was Teysin Gompo, and he had yet another in the lamasery. What's in a name? "Raji" came from an experience at an Indian music concert, wherein I was drawn back to Tibet by the cadence of the drum, and recollected most of the details of Raji's early life and career. He was called "Rajahadikrishnan" by the Indians. And since "Raji" is easier than the other mouthful in everyday speech, it became his tag, label, name. My close friends know who I mean when I say "Raji." What else matters?

Little did I know that this tiny view of him at Dori's was to be the first crack of the Western egg, the first chick-peep of the ancient world giving voice, the beginning of my Eastern odyssey that would end up in vegetarianism and adherence to the tenets of Hinduism and Buddhism.

India began to call me, and Egypt, and Phoenicia, and Crete. Recognition came that my lifelong fascination with certain foods, smells, and sounds was based on experience of these ancient places. I had repressed a good deal of it, as it was simply not the thing to gad about in white robes chanting *Om* in the neighbourhood I grew up in. They'd think you were a Hare Krishna "like those awful

Beatles." (Whom I loved. Especially George.) I had seen the ridicule to which my neighbours across the street, followers of Yogananda, had been put. I was enough of a far-out weird hippie child already without enduring that, thanks.

I began channeling regularly at this time, though I was and am too lazy to meditate with any regularity. I started first with the Ouija board, because that's what I was using, but it quickly became too slow. I heard the voices in my head anyway; the board was just a focal point. But I was loath to give up this crutch, else people would think it was *I* who was speaking, rather than Them. I wore out a couple of boards in this time, and Kevin made me a lovely one, which he carved and painted to my specifications. The letters were Greek-style; it had a pentagram, the cauldron of rebirth, a three-armed spiral, and the eternal circle of the sun/moon. You couldn't get much more cross-cultural. It was painted a very pale yellow, with dark-green lettering and trim. The two colours which were "mine."

But I did give the board up, eventually, as it was just too cumbersome and slow and, I realized, pointless. What did I care where people thought "it" was coming from? The information was the same. As Einstein said, "Where do you think imagination comes from [but 'God']?"

I channeled past-life information, overleaf information, prospects for various people's endeavours, but my real area of interest was the nature of the universe, the nature of reality. Old soul stuff. As I've said, as a child, I always wanted to be dead because then I would Know. Out of the mouths of babes and sucklings. I knew what I was talking about, way back when.

But very few of our orthodox circle knew all this. On the surface I was merely a single-parent college student—politically radical and I dressed funny, but college students often do, especially in San Francisco. And then I was merely little wifey, bringing up two little boys. I made period costumes, but taking in sewing was acceptable. I certainly didn't tell anyone at the prep school where Kevin worked (for the Jesuits) that I channeled a mid Astral Plane entity, and understood that this little planet and the universe was far, far older than we all were brought up to believe! No way! They still had a difficult time integrating Darwin. This was way out of their league.

Channeling on the board, and then off it, was really no different from listening to Them as I had done my whole life. I was merely giving voice to The Voice. But it did take the development of a few muscles, as it were. When I first began using the board, the words came very slow. This, I was told, was due to resistance—mine!—and the editing of information inherent in transmission in such a manner. As Cathleen later put it, regarding the efficacy of channels and forms of channeling, there's a crystal set and state-of-the-art stereo: the information is the same; it's the clarity and level of detail that vary.

I also tired fairly quickly in the early days, especially when I began doing straight transmission without the board. Fifteen minutes was about my limit. If I went beyond this I would get headaches. This is known in New Age literature as a "psychic headache," and requires some grounding—and a little common sense! (Not something Warriors are famous for when it comes to our bodies; we tend to wear them out)—to avoid.

Then the inverse happened: I began to be able to go for longer periods, but I would be so wired that I wouldn't be able sleep at night. This too, has leveled out with time. Now I can go into a good trance, do channeling for about an hour, or maybe two, and get up as if from a nice nap. And I have recall of the information, which not everybody does. Though if the information has been dense, or the "time" reach "far" back, the substance evaporates quickly. This is why it's good to have someone taking notes, or a tape recorder.

Kevin was my note-taker for a long time, pleasing to his Scholar soul. They like picayune detail work like note-taking and cartography. Not we Warriors. (Merriwether Lewis must have been a Scholar to William Clark's adventuresome Warrior.) As my friend Emily Baumbach—a Michael channel—has written of Warriors: "To hell with details, give me results!" Eventually, the sheer volume of information wore even my trusty Scholar out: we began having people bring tapes whenever possible, or at least their own pencils and paper.

With some people, I still do get wired. I remember the first person I really noticed it with. The priest who married Kevin and me had just read the Michael books when we met, and we spent some time talking about the information. When Cameron came up from Los Angeles for the wedding we spent time together, and I was zinging, but I thought it was the wedding. When he came to visit the following December, I knew it was *him*; he came for a Scottish breakfast at half-past ten, stayed for three or four hours, and at two A.M. I still could not sleep. Reason: he's an entity mate of mine with whom I have a very strong connection. We really do plug each other in.

All through this period I was working on my own past, cataloguing as many lifetimes as I could recall, with the intention of working them up into stories, and eventually a book about digging up past lives (a current work-in-progress), much as standard genealogists do. The data and methods are all the same. The only difference is the use to which they are put. I wondered sometimes what the little old ladies I sat beside at our local genealogical library would think if they knew I was delving into the Skelton family of Virginia or the MacLeods of Skye because I had been of those families in the 18th or 16th centuries. Probably that I was as fruity as great-Aunt Mabel, whom they locked up in the attic, and no one ever talked about. Such ruminations didn't stop me from my research: *I knew* what was so, and I was determined to validate my knowledge.

But I did not cross the line into frankness. Or, at least not often. One of the times I did was with my midwifery teacher, and Liz accepted it with the grace of the Leo lady she is.

I had long wanted to be a midwife. I had Lelia's experience, and that of many others in the past, urging me to it. When I was pregnant with Rudraigh I had been with the certified nurse-midwives at San Francisco General, and the woman teaching the childbirth preparation course was herself a traditional midwife (and had been trained by my midwifery teacher, Liz Davis). Rifka urged me to become an R.N., as the political situation in California made it difficult for traditional midwives to practice. She wanted to spare me that difficulty. But I wanted to do it the old way, *the way I remembered.* Stubborn old Warrior.

When I was in the waiting room of our pediatrician's office when my second son Cian was an infant, I found my opportunity: a flyer was sitting on the table announcing up-coming midwifery intensives given by author and San Francisco midwife, Elizabeth Davis. It was galvanizing. Come hell or high water, I would do it, over and above Kevin's considerable objections. "We believe," he told a student of his, using the royal pronoun, "that the mother should stay home for the first five years of a child's life." And he was savvy enough to know what odd hours midwifery would require of me; to say nothing of the political situation. I could in theory be arrested for practicing medicine without a license. But, with my Irish experience behind me, that was not a daunting fear.

When I met Liz, I had the familiar *I know you* reaction, which, from the look she gave me, I believe was mutual. By the end of the first day, I had sifted out from where and was emboldened to tell her, "I have done this [midwifery] before, with you. In Crete."

Crete. Long, sun-drenched days in the Minoan temple, where I was dedicated as a priestess to Britomaris Aphrodite. We took care of ourselves in those days, and did more than accept offerings in the name of the goddess from passing men. Temple ritual has a very bad reputation, thanks to Christianity, and I expect the popular image of the "temple prostitute"—a Salome—will never be eradicated from the public mind. But in those days we did more than play the goddess. We were healers, spiritually and bodily, of all who came to us. There were not many children born to us devotees of the temple, for we had our means of birth control (*not* infanticide, as is popularly imagined), but once in a while there would be a birth. It was never an "oops." For this, we had training in childbirth. And Liz was one of the Old Ones, the initiators, the teachers. A sort of pre-Christian Mother Abbess (though that's likely to get me branded for blasphemy). She has been my teacher in this regard several times since, and I will always regard her as such, even when we are very old, disembodied and One. My respect and fealty are founded in long old experience.

It was because of Liz's course that I met Cathleen. Cathleen was teaching childbirth preparation at St. Elizabeth's and Liz sent her former students Cathleen's way as labour coaches for the girls.

The first time I heard Cathleen's name, I knew I knew her, that we had practiced together before—would again—and that our relationship would be very important to my life. But it was like my telling Wendy I knew that I would find my destiny in San Francisco: how little I realized the implications of those words when spoken! For Cathleen had been in Crete, too. Cathleen had been my aunt and teacher Moira in Ireland. Cathleen is an entity mate of mine and has been in nearly every lifetime with me in some regard. We are comrades-in-arms, Warriors both, and she was to unlock for me the whole treasure-trove of the ancient world and facilitate the future I have enacted in Williamsburg.

Chapter Six

ॐ

A Little Help From My Friends; or, Ancient Rimes

I had an image of Cathleen in my mind before I met her at St. Elizabeth's: tall, rangy, dark-haired, looking rather like the Welsh actress Sian Phillips, or Maud Gonne in old age. This expected image was reinforced by her voice in our telephone conversation. What I found the first night of labour classes was a tall, well-built dark blonde, looking rather like the English model Patty Boyd (George Harrison's first wife). It was a shock. *You look different!*

What I was looking for, resonating with, of course was Moira in Ireland, and she was there, is there, peeps out with regularity. But then, so do all the rest of Cat's "characters," depending on what's resonating currently. So do mine.

Moira O'Kett was as unsentimental a person as you could hope to find in the mid-17th century in a tiny village in the west of Ireland. Highly skilled, critically observant, possessed of a razor-edged wit, she dispensed what is currently known as "tough love." She was not without compassion, but she was never one to suffer fools gladly. She never married—Cathleen says that all the men in the village were afraid of her, and, by my memory, I agree—but took lovers as she chose, generally men passing through who were not overawed by her reputation. She lived alone, an independent woman; that is, a virgin in its original sense. She was magnificent. Lelia admired her greatly, revered her, though she was too unsentimental to say so.

They were very alike. Cathleen and I still are. We are not identically matched, but we have the same sense of things, the same reactions, and so it was with Lelia and Moira. Cathleen is softer of heart than Moira, more uncertain of having all the answers, but that comes with the soul's aging. The more you know, the more you know you don't know.

The Irish connection was bubbling when we met because of the circumstances. There we were, doing midwifery again, she the authority (and later equal, but still revered). There has to be a primary resonance to get the "new" connection going, and Clare was ours. Under other circumstances, the resonance might have been Kansas, Scotland, India, Rome, Egypt, or Crete, to name a few places we've hung out together.

Our foray into the completely weird this time around occurred when, after one of the first labour classes, Cathleen was pondering aloud as to how to proceed in her midwifery course. Should she do an apprenticeship? Cave in and take an R.N.? She said she wished she knew someone who read [tarot] cards or something. Whereupon, I said, "I do!" I brought them the next week, and in the darkened foyer of St. E's after class we laid the cards on the table, in more ways than one.

"We've done this together before, you know," I said, looking at the spread. We looked at one another.

"What do you mean?" she asked. Dear sister, I will remember that moment for ever!

"In Ireland," I continued. "You were my teacher." I saw Moira's face in hers, a double image, as I have so easily done with people my life long. I needed no one to tell me, and no one could dissuade me from my knowing.

St. E's found us another member of the circle of that life. Janet was a labour coach likewise, and Cathleen at first found her a little hard to take, but didn't know why. She was a perfectly nice person, cheerful, friendly, open. One evening we found out why. Janet was in the nurse's station waiting for Cat to arrive, and when she did, wearing a Kinsale (Irish) cloak which I had made for her, Janet stared at her and said, "I've seen you wearing that before!"

Cathleen, who knew by her look that she meant Before (as she had never worn it in front of her in our current time-frame) was a little nonplussed to hear this coming from Janet in the middle of the (albeit empty) nurse's station at a Catholic institution. Nevertheless, she replied with aplomb, "It's Irish. Kelly made it for me."

"We've been midwives together," Janet said, persisting.

Faintly, in the ethers, came the music from "The Twilight Zone," for by then we had shared our memories, and Cathleen *knew* Janet had been her apprentice then, another niece. And she hadn't liked her.

When I came in later, wearing my Kinsale cloak (my winter "coat"), Janet exclaimed, "You have one, too!"

"One what?" says I, like a dope.

"An Irish cloak."

"Yeah," I drawled, throwing my belongings into a chair. "I made it. And Cathleen's."

Then I was apprised of the former conversation.

My internal reaction was less than overjoyed. More like *OH-MYGODNOTYOUAGAIN!* as cousin Gillian—Gillie—had been everything Lelia was not, in many regards: tiny, dainty, with midnight black hair and very white skin, blue eyes, a sweet figure, voice like a linnet, she made one feel coarse and cow-like. Lelia was tall and broad and freckled ("a great large woman" as they say admiringly in West Clare), the sort of woman who could push a plow and heave turf and mend a fence. Not exactly dainty and ladyish.

But Gillie was also lazy, inept, daydreaming, and spiteful. "You'd have to nag her all day to get the herbs ground and then she'd whine all while doing it," as Cathleen recalls. She was not fit to be a midwife, had no interest in it. She'd been sent to Mor only to keep her out of trouble in her village, where she was wreaking havoc amongst the young men. She was the one who was responsible for Lelia's being accused of witchcraft and worse, because she thought I was garnering too much prestige, and she wanted a little for herself.

With all this roiling around in my head, I made some lame response and then was hit with Janet's query as to whether, being interested in past lives, I'd read the Michael books. Aha! a fellow initiate! Talk about a tangled knot of reactions and emotions! I've since forgiven Janet for Gillie's spite, and love her well, but it took a while to work through.

Cat and I spent long hours wading through various resonances and comparing experiences of recollections, but this was only after we waded through her enculturation by the Jehovah's Witnesses that such things were of the devil and her reluctance to be thought a nut. She says I was very patient with her million questions, but I had an ulterior purpose, for I knew that she knew this stuff, if she would only let go of fear and open up to it. Thus I was a little zealous and (Chief Feature coming in) impatient with her at times. Not the best of teachers. But I did know that I could not convince her of what I and she knew, no matter how many ways I explained it, or what she herself knew. Acceptance, belief, had to come from within her.

These came slowly. The universe never gives us more than we can deal with at once, no matter how it may sometimes seem when we are overwhelmed by resonances and happenings and wonder if we are teetering on the edge of sanity.

Sometimes, her view of a particular lifetime was radically (and intriguingly) different from mine. We have shared every possible human relationship, as either sex, and, as I've said, the personality persists through "time."

In Scotland in the late 16th century she was my kinsman, my cousin. I was then the sister of the Chief of Clan MacLeod—Margaret—and she was his Chieftain on the Isle of Lewis, Torquil. She (then he) was married to the sister of Margaret's husband, Donald Gorm Mor MacDonald of Sleat, a woman also named Margaret. There was no love lost between Margaret MacLeod and her husband Donald MacDonald, and clan annals are full of tales of their "domestic friction," hence my view of Donald has always been somewhat jaundiced.

When Cathleen began talking about being on campaign with Donald, or drinking in the Great Hall, I had an entirely different view of him as a greatly respected warrior (and rake). And woe betide me when she gave forth with Torquil's view of Margaret—either of them—or women in general! It was unsentimental and entirely unsympathetic. Basically, it was Torquil's opinion that if we hadn't been such nagging bitches, life would have been a lot more pleasant for everybody. We were our own worst enemies. All that he and Donald, or any man, wanted was a little peace and quiet, a soft answer instead of a shrill, and a comely kiss instead of a wicked left hook. You didn't see the village girls behaving that way; they were much more fun to be with. Who wanted to live with a shrew?

Oh, I learned right well what the collective male opinion of Margaret was, for I heard the fireside complaints and advice from Cathleen. Such revelations at 400 years' distance are still a bit "ouchy," but I recognize their truth, and they helped me gain a more balanced view of life in the Hebrides than I had on my own. I hope I did the same for Cat by putting forth the ladies' case.

At any rate, we had (and continue to have) great fun reminiscing about Highland Scotland. A pair of old folks trading war stories, sometimes poignant, sometimes funny, often extremely insightful concerning our present personalities and relationship difficulties. And it had other uses: for the next Renaissance Faire, I gave her a length of the dark MacLeod tartan to wear as a plaidy. (Precursor to the modern kilt. Worn as the Great Belted Plaid by men and as a sort of shawl-cloak by women.) Disregarding that there were no "clan" tartans as we know them in the 16th century, it was a way of making a connection to the past that was tangible. (Though I have not subjected her to a meal of the dreaded haggis. There are some things she won't do even for our friendship's sake, and eating haggis is one of them.)

There was another resonance we shared which for me had a profound impact. She spoke of her life as a Witness, and the familiarity the ancient world they studied from the Bible had for her. She could remember temple service, and never thought it particularly wicked, though she had been told it was.

Crete. Crete. Crete. It thrummed in my head. *She was there, too. With me. With Liz.* I saw her as she was then, waiting with me in the courtyard on festival days to be chosen. The sun was warm, the dates sweet. Sweeter still our hashish-laced honey wine. Flashes came: lying in the sun, laughing together, being massaged with fragrant oils. We were well-pampered in our service to the Goddess.

The Goddess. . .because of her position as teacher to scores of midwives, Liz was known affectionately amongst Bay Area midwives as The Goddess. Her elegant and benign character fit this appellation also. I told Cathleen of my remark to Liz at the first class.

"Yes!" she exclaimed. She knew, also. A door had been opened. Another life spent with my comrade, my sister, my entity-mate. Many were the hours we spent culling the gems of memory of everyday life in Minoan Crete. These were later verified in archaeology books Kevin brought home for me. And in classical mythology. Minos, Theseus, Icarus, and Daedalus were no more mere "mythological" figures.

I tuned into Crete once to discern my name and family history, and recalled that my name was Car (but Cybele was my temple name). I was of Athenian origin, of medium height, with honey-coloured hair and eyes and tawny skin; I had been a twin; I was dedicated to temple service at an early age, and was removed from my family; my father had made little wooden votive offerings (among other things) for the king.

The last rang a bell in my head, and I looked up the information on votive offerings in *Bullfinch's Mythology. DAEDALUS MADE WOODEN VOTIVE OFFERINGS FOR MINOS, THE KING OF CRETE!!!!*

It was mind-blowing. I had read of Daedalus and Icarus, but never knew he made such votive offerings. Now the game was afoot. Going further, I looked up Car. She was a fertility goddess of the Mediterranean, patroness of the Aegean; Icarus, or, Icarius, was her devotee.

Now I was perplexed. Which came first, the chicken or the egg? Had we/I been named for these heroes and goddesses? Or were we the genesis of their cult? It is something for which I have not yet an answer.

What I know is that one day while nearing the end of my time in active service a young man with golden-brown hair chose me to enact the ritual with him. As was the custom, we did not speak our names. We enacted the ritual and he afterwards went off for private prayers, as did I. I did not see him again. Later, I went out into the common area where the offerings were left by those who had done service that day. I saw some little wooden votives there, and a shudder ran through me. Memory beckoned. My father had made such little wooden offerings. I had not seen them in almost twenty years. I asked my temple-sister [Cathleen], who was standing by, who left them.

"Oh," she said, rolling her eyes, "a very handsome young fellow with golden brown hair, quite tall. . ." and she went on to describe the young man I had been with. Realization struck like a stone: *It was my brother, Icarus.* We had not recognised one another.

There was no stigma, no shame in it, for how were we to know? The goddess had her own plans, for a child came of that ritual (rare, and suspicious in itself, for we generally used little carved pessaries during our fertile time—and I was by all signs not at that time) and he was dedicated to temple service from birth. We called him Icarius.

I cannot answer whether I was Car or named for her; but suddenly, I had answers to questions every archaeologist and paleoethnologist dreams about. I can be certain, based on my previous experiences of knowing what had occurred before in places I had never been in this lifetime, that someday the scholars will verify what I know.

So it was that the ancient world began to beckon.

I had studied Roman and Greek history as an adjunct to Celtic studies—as all the early views we have of the Celts are by the classical authors—and I knew of a couple of lifetimes in Greece and Rome. But I never paid it much mind. I knew all that stuff. Livy. Plutarch. Cousin Claudius, and that rotten little Caligula. Yeah yeah. Old hat. Yawn.

But Crete was "way back," in the Early Bronze Age. 1500 B.C. Minoan Crete was exotic, Middle Eastern in flavour. Crete was the centre of the world, with its contacts with Greece, Egypt, and the Middle East. From Crete, it was a mere frog-leap to Phoenicia— where I was also in temple service—to Syria, to Egypt, to East

Africa. . .to . . .I didn't have a name for before that. Except Atlantis, and that still felt hokey. *We didn't call it that. Or Lemuria either.*

WHERE DID THAT COME FROM? My head was really spinning. But it was only the beginning.

I went to Cathleen's, and she was playing music from the Tutankhamen Exhibit. Egypt had always called her. Sitting in her dining room, listening to her outpouring of vivid tales of childhood in the court of Ahkenaton, I saw again the physician I was.

That's when that was. We were there together.

But still Cathleen doubted. How did she know this wasn't all just fantasy, as her husband said? Listen, I said, if this is fantasy, then it's mass hallucination. I told her about my physician. I'd never told anyone about my Egyptian physician, as it was too close to being a stereotypical past-life belief. But I knew I was safe with Cathleen.

The resonances were coming thick and fast, and we began to realize how often we had been together. How often all of us had been together, how very much we traveled in packs, the same group over and over again, with different faces, bodies, personalities, relationships to each other. As far as "belief" went, Cathleen was about to have her denouement, and it would have a profound effect on my entire way of life.

She has a friend with whom she has always felt a strong connection, but could never articulate exactly why. India has always called her. One night, the pieces of the puzzle came together.

She was lying in the tub with candles and incense burning,

and suddenly she was not in her tub in San Francisco, but in India, sharing a ritual bath with her young husband on their wedding night. Their families were spice merchants, and it was an arranged marriage. She was very young; her husband was young also, but older than she. His name was Vanda, and he played the sitar. Hers was Indra, and she was everything an Indian wife should be, soft of manner and submissive to her husband. It was sometime in the mid 5th century A.D. And she suddenly knew what the connection was with her friend. They had been married in India. Her lingering doubts about "all this stuff" dissolved under the impact of the recognition, and the fulfillment of this life-long resonance.

As she told me about the experience, and the details of the life, I kept thinking that it sounded all too familiar. When she spoke of Vanda's sisters, collectively known as "the aunties," and their cosseting of her, their gossip sessions, I had the weird sense of knowing what she was going to say. That gaggle of plump, middle-aged women were as vivid and clear in my memory as anything that I had ever seen. For the first time in my life they were clearly in focus, and my fascination with Indian people and culture made sense. I had for so long followed with hungry eyes the path of sari-and-cardigan clad old Indian women without knowing why, and frequently declared that I found Indian women the most beautiful creatures. All of which I'm sure seemed inexplicable to those around me.

I suppressed this realization for a long time, did not tell anyone how strong the resonance to the East was becoming. It was patently absurd; here I was, a Celtic scholar, the prototypical colleen, yearning after India. Would I make myself ridiculous, as those English ladies who, under the British Raj, went native and wore the white drapery of the devotee? Cathleen was the only one who knew, and she fostered the connection with tea and music and cookery books. (I suffered from cravings for dal and curry and chapatis, the food of a place always being a primary source of resonance.)

But even she could not bring forth the most obvious connotation of that lifetime. The realization that Padme had not always been one of the roly-poly, comfortable "aunties" had to come from me.

One day I was in my kitchen, reaching up on one of my herb shelves for something, and—bam!—without warning found myself standing in our shop in Agra as a young girl, reaching up likewise, for a stalk of dried red berries. The arm that reached was narrow and smooth as a carob branch, draped in a brilliantly dyed sari of orange that was exquisitely trimmed in purple and gold. Padme was short. Too short to reach what she required, and behind her up came a young man—her cousin and fiancee, Amani, who was working in the shop that day. He laid his hand upon her shoulder chidingly, shaking his head at her struggles on tiptoe, then reached up and fetched down the berries himself. The scene retreated a little, and I could see them both standing there, and Padme was as slim and young and beautiful as the girl in *The Jungle Book*. I was shocked. *Padme had once been young! And slim!* Up till then my only recollection of her was in middle age, near the time of her death. It may seem obvious that she would of course once have been young and slim, but it was not to me. It was akin to a child seeing a picture of his grandparent as a teenager; disorienting to my reality.

In that I was not alone. Kevin knew about Tibet. He tolerated my forays to Tibet Day and would on occasion turn up a book on Tibetan Buddhism for me. I think he was amused at the shift from my anti-Eastern stance (Raji had been thunked on the head—and killed—by a passing Mongol horde, and anything Chinese gave me a headache—including food) to such an adherence to it, but I don't know that he realized about India, until I came home with yards and yards of ochre cotton for the plain sari of a devotee. Changes were happening in me, and to me, for which he was really unprepared. Where was the Maeve he was first attracted to? She had become more of a hermit monk than a woman warrior. He didn't like it, but he never complained much. Except about the music. Tibetan chant and Indian ragas are not his thing. As I joked to a colleague of mine in Williamsburg, Tibetan chant was the death-knell to my marriage. I was Becoming, and we were drifting apart.

My semi-vegetarianism was burgeoning into the real thing. I never forced it on him, or my children, and continued to cook what they were used to, but for myself took on more of the material culture and beingness of the East.

I began collecting the works of masters and holy men—from Lao Tzu to the current Dalai Lama; names long familiar were sought out—reverberations at long last of my fascination with those neighbours of ours who were followers of Yogananda, with the Hare Krishnas I met with in the Haight Ashbury and in airports. I had never spurned them, mocked them as so many of my acquaintances did, but accepted their gifts of flowers gratefully, for in their way of being I recognised something I knew. Admitting it was the hard part, for I had vociferously denied any interest in the East, and now "suddenly" here I was, turning in earnest to Buddhist, Hindu, and Taoist texts and meditation.

My yoga class in college, with its end-of-term report on Baba Ram Dass' book _Journey of Awakening_, was less an aberration to anyone observant enough to see the change. It was one more step on a long path. In the Eastern way, the Middle Path, I had at last come truly home. Full circle. I had traversed the road of memory from the modern world to the ancient, from West to East, and was ready for a place of no dogma and no direction but Expansion into the Infinite. The desire for Liberation had come, an end to my fascination with life on the physical plane. It had been fun, but I was done with it. The soul desire now was to move on to the higher planes.

All this Cathleen had facilitated, and when I say that I owe her a good deal, this is what I mean, for had it not been for her own awakening I would not have suffered mine. She moved me a far piece along my path, and for that she literally has my eternal gratitude. But as she would likely say of it, that's what entity-mates are for. We're a family, and we aid and comfort one another.

Chapter Seven

ॐ

Saturday Evening Post; or, Do You Want to Know a Secret

After the experience of my childhood and young adulthood, I was in no way eager to tell the world at large what I in my heart believed, and so spent the first several years of my marriage keeping all my secrets to myself (with some notable exceptions), denying, like one accused of witchcraft, that I believed anything extraordinary at all. I was, after all, the wife of a tenured faculty member of a Catholic prep school, and our son Rudraigh later went to a parochial school, further entangling me in the persona of the good Catholic wife and mother. Mark me, I have nothing against the Church. I still do attend Mass, for it yet has the capability send me soaring to heavenly bliss, particularly during High Mass, for I was a Christian monk several times and the resonance is sweet. I still do believe in the divinity of Jesus Christ. But as the poet William Blake said when asked likewise if he believed that Christ was God personified, "I believe He was God. But so am I. And so are you."

But it was never intended that I should have a nice quiet little life, pretending to be your everyday ordinary Catholic, meanwhile believing in the interconnectedness of all things, reincarnation and so forth. Heaven forbid I should have admitted I was drawn to Buddhism! Never mind that our neighbourhood, and Rudraigh's school, had become largely Chinese (to my Tibetan monk, it was living amongst the enemy, rather like his modern-day counterparts in Lhasa today); the bulk of them were firmly Christians of one stripe or another. And there was too much in me, lurking beneath the surface, that wanted expression for that. I had thought I could get away with merely writing about various experiences, past and present, as fiction, and leave it at that. Had not Taylor Caldwell and others done so successfully?

I should have known it was not possible in college, at Wendy's house, when I was taken back to the County Clare on hearing the Chieftains. I should have known with Molly. I should have known a hundred times over, and yet I hoped to pass as normal. This sprang from fear of persecution, fear of ridicule, fear of rejection, and fear alone. As Michael, and Irene, have said: there are only two forces in the universe, Love and Fear. How true it is!

The first outsider I told of my view of reality was the priest who married us—a Jesuit who read tarot cards, and had a few weird experiences of his own. Looking back on it now, I don't think Cameron, with his bagpipes and tartan vestments, really counted as telling an outsider, for it was preaching to the choir. He had read the Michael books, brought up that he had read them, asked me if I knew anything of them. (This conversation we got to by way of discussing why Kevin and I wanted texts from ancient pagan Celtic folktales as our readings rather than Gospel texts.) But admitting my beliefs to Cameron, representing as he did the established Church (though there were a few old priests who thought he ought to be excommunicated for reading cards), was a great leap of faith to me at the time. And it was a great relief that he understood me. Not many else had. Contrary to what might be assumed of folklorists and other anthropologists, my teachers, fellow students, and colleagues did not necessarily believe what they were reading and collecting from "contacts" about the Otherworld. This is known as maintaining professional skepticism, objectivity (or plain humbug).

I was the subject of informal, and quite amused, study by the director of our anthropology museum, who, when I returned from Ireland with my tale of having met Michael Kilbride (Mick Rafferty as was) in Dublin, leaned back in his chair, puffed on his pipe thoughtfully a moment, stroked his beard, then asked me in all seriousness if I thought this was a case of The Daemon Lover. [This is a famous folklore motif wherein the (usually deceased) lover returns to entice the woman away from her new husband and baby, only to lure her to her death "accidentally," usually at sea. The Child Ballads contain a song—"House Carpenter"—made very popular by Joan Baez in the '60s, which illustrates this motif.]

Talk about being under glass! I felt like a bug, a Zulu, a Maori under his wry gaze. I point out that this was a man who thought me pretty weird anyway, and had given me a Valentine's card with myself pictured on the front as the ancient British queen Boudicca (or, Boadicea if you're veddy British). I guess he thought anything was possible as far as I was concerned.

One of the very rare exceptions to my silence—a situation in which I was bound to tell the truth for my own sake—occurred just after we had returned from Ireland. I was fed up to the teeth with waiting for Kevin to make up his mind about our relationship, so when no permanent proposals of any kind were forthcoming in Ireland or after (and I would have settled for living together for he was at this point yet living at home), I decided three years was long enough, and it was time to cut my losses. From then on, we had a child in common, no more. It was in this state of mind, of being mistress of my own affairs again (so to speak) that I went to work at the Renaissance Pleasure Faire in northern California. That year I gained entry into the Clan Colin—the Scottish Highlanders—St. Brigid's Guild, into which I had always desired membership, for my memories of several lifetimes in Scotland are strong, and that in the Hebrides in the late 1500s particularly. I had always "played Faire" with them, had been asked on occasion to officially join their number, but never was brave enough. The more unpleasant resonances of Margaret's life (read on!) kept me from it.

At the time, I was teaching archery up in the middle of the Faire, a serious job which I enjoyed, but which gave me no real time to "play Faire," the inmates' term for roaming the site and engaging in witty repartee with other costumed interpreters and visitors. Nevertheless, I had a character then, for my jaunts about: Ailish ni-Cruailleach—Elizabeth Crowley; a midwife.

In that little shire of Chipping-Under-Oakwood there were many activities. We even had a visit from Queen Elizabeth I, making her one of her Royal Progresses through the countryside (which the genuine article did several times through England, staying at the homes of the great nobles and bankrupting them in their efforts to provide her with suitable quarters, victuals, and entertainments). "Queen's Prog," as we called it, occurred at half-past two in the afternoon, as she made her way in a litter from the entrance gate to the Ben Johnson stage at the top of the Faire, and there held Court.

Among her honour guard every day were the clansmen of the Scots' Camp, armed to the teeth and showing off their fine weapons and handsome tartans—not to mention knees—along the way. They were not especially loyal to the Queen as a group, as for many years they had literally been beyond the beyonds—relegated to setting up their camp outside the bounds of Faire proper, but they were always eager—as were their genuine predecessors—for a display of clan pride.

All work stopped while the Queen passed by, and obeisances were made to her. This I found generally irksome, as my persona, my character, was never English; I had been Cornish or Welsh, but as a Celticist never considered them to be English. So it was that I made my curtseys with no little disdain, and always cheered when the Irish under Eoghan Roe O'Neill, the Earl of Tyrone, came past, followed by the Scots of the Clan Colin.

One day, I looked up from my curtsey to find myself being regarded in a very familiar fashion by one of the men of the Clan. He had long, golden-brown curls and ice-blue eyes, and when I met those eyes I was petrified. I do not know how long he had been looking at me, for Faire was by this time several weeks into its run. But a wash of cold dread and recognition passed through me. I knew him as surely as I knew my own name, and I knew from where!

Scotland. 1596.

This was the lifetime in the Isle of Skye, the wife of Donald Gorm Mor MacDonald of Sleat, Chief of the great Clan Donald, Pretender to the Lordship of the Isles; and the sister of the Isle's other great Chief, Rory Mor MacLeod. These two men were by turns allies (never real *friends*) and mortal enemies. What transpired due to the alliance—cemented by Margaret and Donald's marriage—is known as the last great clan war between the MacLeods and the Mac-Donalds on the Isle of Skye.

Donald's ghost—Clan Donald legend has it—drove successive generations of MacDonalds from their castle at Duntulm with his terrifying activities. In mortal life he was a monster who, in repayment for some minor transgression, threw one of his own kinsmen down the dungeons at Duntulm, which are below sea level, and shut him up solid for a week with no food or water. After a week, he tossed down some salt beef and closed the hatch, never to be reopened while the man lived. His screams were heard all over the policy of the castle. And archaeology bears witness to the tales that he clawed his fingers to bloody stumps in the granite walls before he died, mad, desperately trying to escape.

My first recollections of that lifetime were of terrific rows between Margaret and Donald, and that she had been accused of witchcraft and infanticide. She had not wanted to be married to the MacDonald, and such activities were her revenge upon him. I have previously noted the remark made by Isabel Fraser-Grant in her *MacLeods, the History of a Clan* that there was between Margaret and Donald "much domestic friction." Honey, I thought, you don't know the half of it!

All this was in my mind when yon bonny Scotsman came after returning from Queen's Prog to "speak a word" with me. My first instinct was to run like the devil, avoid him at all cost. The trouble was that he was charming, very charming, as even Donald could be sometimes. Now, I was used to admiring looks, suggestive remarks, and assorted gropes from both participants and visitors by this time, having worked the Faire since I was sixteen years old in either northern or southern California. Simple lusty interest I could handle; I could easily put off the admirer, if not with sweet charm then with scathing directness. But this was different. There was a sense of compulsion, even obsession about it, of being drawn into the situation against one's will, which is signal of the karmic nature of such relationships. And physical attraction is a very enticing lure. Were it not for physical attraction, many of us would never entangle ourselves in relationships to which we have agreed to work out imbalances, otherwise known as karmic debts. I was taken in by "Donald's" charm, as Margaret never was.

My reaction to the situation vacillated wildly between desire and dread, purely physical on the one hand and wholly spiritual on the other. Part of me wanted to settle the imbalance, cancel the debt; part of me was terrified of a repeat of the scene in Skye.

Finally, hoping to avoid the entire situation, I confronted him one night after closing, with words that would either blow his mind— make him think I was a complete nut and hence make him go away—or trigger some memory, however vague, and fill him with as much dread as I had, and hence make him go away.

The sun was declining beyond the Napa hills, and people were already out with lanterns and flashlights. There was a chill in the air as I stood before him in front of the great Tudor facade of the archery booth and said in a manner I hoped was portentous, "The last time I knew you, you were Donald MacDonald of Sleat."

He didn't get it.

To my dismay, he only bridled with arrogant pleasure, which is exactly what he would have done then, for the MacDonald was a vain man. Some people never change.

Suffice it to say that the situation was not avoided, for he bumbled into it without the sense God gave a goat, and I gritted my teeth, gave over my dread, hoped for the best and played the scene.

I was told in no uncertain terms by the Laird of the Clan that "Donald"—who was one of his chieftains, and Captain of the guards—was as dear to him as a son, and he would not see him made unhappy. I was as much as ordered to *handfast* to him, which we did; as Margaret and Donald did, as I had known and validated in my research.

Handfasting is an ancient custom dating back to the time of the Picts, a form of marriage which was recognised as a legal bond in Scotland until the mid-1970s. It is a contract between two people or clans, requiring only the officiation of a clan chief—or, as tradition has it, "in dire circumstances" only the consent of the couple. Properly done, the pair come together, each led by a group of men or women—representing the community—before the chief (or laird). Consent is asked and given, the dowry of both is read out, gifts exchanged, and the pair step over the laird's sword which is drawn and laid on the ground before them. The contract is for a year and a day (forever to the Celtic mind, for all of eternity is made up of the turning of night into day, and the whole cycle of seasons), at the end of which time the pair may decide to stay together or part as they choose.

We were handfasted in great ceremony, and I was asked whether this was "for real or for Faire." In the most profound way, I had to say it was for real. Immediately I was assaulted with an oppressive sense of dread. Memories of Margaret's unhappiness and her public humiliation at the hands of her unwanted husband were saying loud and clear, "Last time, you went along with what was planned for you like a docile lamb, and look what happened. Get out now while you still can!" This time, I listened. This time, I followed my instincts. Our little contract was not a fortnight old before I repudiated it.

We were due at a gathering of the clans for Highland Games the next week, to publicly acknowledge the handfasting and hence my captain's advancement in the Clan hierarchy. Steeling myself, knowing what my words would entail for me, I told "Donald" that I abrogated our handfast. I don't remember what lame excuse I gave, but he accepted it with great difficulty. The Games would now be for him a public humiliation, tantamount to being left at the altar or having your lady run off with the gypsies, as it goes in the folksong. The karmic scale was balanced, but not with any consciousness on his part.

For my part, I was kin-wrecked, shunned, banished from the Clan until the old Laird departed much afterward and his coterie with him. Such was how seriously matters were taken at Faire. It was a little world all unto its own. By that time, however, my "Donald" was long gone from the Faire, working in Alaska, I heard tell. I felt very bad. Not for being kin-wrecked so much as for causing him such pain. But I could not endure the scenes of Skye again. Often and often I have thought, "If only he had heeded my words at first, and never pressed matters!" To my mind, I gave him fair warning. I know it is difficult for most people to understand why I would handfast with—"marry"—him in the first place, and then renege, and the only answer I can give is that we had an old score to settle and our higher selves knew well what we were doing, if our conscious selves did not and viewed the proceedings as irrational. But such is how we learn.

Lesson One: Just because you tell people doesn't mean they'll hear you.

Parenthetically, Kevin and I got back together at this point, though he had not been really aware that we were apart until a misunderstanding caused the horrific scene of "Donald" coming home with me after one Faire weekend. (He said he needed a ride to SF so he could catch the bus back home, being without a car at the moment; naively, I thought he meant just that.) I ought to point out here that Kevin was in Scotland then too, as our seneschal (shanachie, poet-in-residence, bard, scribe) Dughall Mac-Crimmons—-of the great piping family—who went with Margaret to Duntulm when she married Donald. He had no reason to love Donald either, for it was he who is spoken of in clan annals when they say that Donald sent his wife back to her brother, "A one-eyed woman accompanied by a one-eyed man, on a one-eyed horse, followed by a one-eyed dog." The "one-eyed"-ness here speaks not of literal one-eyedness, as one git of an "historian" supposed in recounting the tale, but of "the evil eye," or the "faery glance." In the folk literature there is a character, Balor of the Evil Eye, a great lummox of a fellow, whose gaze is killing. What the tales were saying was that Margaret was accused of being fey—a witch—and was sent back to her brother with the accomplice in her crimes (Dughall), on a faery horse (usually black or dapple grey, sometimes white with red ears) with a faery dog (always white with red ears).

Mythology aside—which Kevin understood perfectly well—he was very kind to me during the awful few weeks during and after the handfasting, for I was pretty close to the edge. The resonances were just a little too strong, the overlap a little too clear. I desperately wanted to get away—went so far as to ring up my friend Mairead in Dublin to ask if I could sleep on her floor for a week; instead I got married. Kevin asked me to choose, offered to marry if I chose him. I did love him, had always wanted to marry him. We had great times, were intellectually extremely well-matched. So I did, overlooking what I should have learned in Ireland. It was a retreat into the safety of normal life, both psychically and materially, as I was worn out with the long struggle of being a single-parent college student, living on grants, student loans, and welfare.

Old souls generally have no love of the daily grind, slugging it out in the business world, struggling to earn a living. In short, we are basically lazy. We like low-stress jobs, like gardening, gas station attending, writing, animal husbandry, babysitting, bumming around. I am no exception. It's not that we expect that the world owes us a living—there can be a tremendous desire for quite humble service in the life—but we *need* to be taken care of while doing it. For those not utterly Realized, it's hard to focus on perfecting your soul when the wolf is at the door. For the Realized, it is no problem. You come to a point when you *really believe,* truly in your soul, that the universe will provide everything you need. Not that your needs are great. You no longer have the desire for excess material goods.

So I got married. I did work for a time, as the head of the crafts department of a fabric store, but then I was pregnant with Cian; the long hours on my feet threatened a miscarriage, and I felt my baby was more important than a job, so I quit. I intended to go back to some kind of work later. (My mother had always worked.) I needed the independence it afforded. I did, with costuming and midwifery, but only at cost to my marriage. But all that was ahead.

My soul urge—if you follow numerology—is for Realization, and service to humanity, and there were some people whom I felt compelled to apprise of my secrets to help bring them along on their own path, open them up to their fullest potential. I count among these several college friends, Wendy included, and Cathleen.

With Cathleen, it was as easy as falling off a log. She had endured the same weird experiences as I and only needed to overcome her enculturated fear of them. For me, answering her thousand and one questions was affirming to what I in fact heard and saw; that it was not crazy, or a product of wishful thinking or possession. It helped clarify in my own mind where I was. This is what teaching is for. You teach what you most want to learn.

With others, it was more like pulling teeth, and though I daresay that certain friends would have come along eventually on their own, there was a lot of impatience and coercion on my part—because I *saw* what they could be *now* in this lifetime, and wanted them to realise themselves. I don't, however, recommend this coercion as a mode of action, especially if the person happens to be of a cynical nature. Rest assured that people will come along as they are intended to without being dragged by you or me, however much we view it for their enlightenment. This is the stuff Inquisitions are made of, and it is definitely not Good Work. (But, if you do find yourself in such a situation, don't beat yourself up about it unnecessarily, either. Everything is a learning process and we aren't expected to be perfect here.)

Sometimes, telling one person can lead to many many others knowing your belief system and an entire path being opened up. So it was with my admitting my world view to the head of the counselling department at Kevin's school. I was not seeking psychoanalysis. She had taught me reike—a form of what was once called "faith healing"—and I was returning the favour by doing a life reading for her, at that time with the aid of my trusty handmade Ouija board. It was a case of telling two friends and them telling two friends, and so on and so on.

The word got out, and the dam overflowed then with a multitude of people, among them Jesuits, faculty members and their spouses, and former students of Kevin's—to say nothing of friends of friends of mine (and their assorted companions)—interested in my experience of hearing voices, seeing ghosts, reading the past, knowing the faeries. I was continually pressed for readings about this person or that, his past lives, how he'd known so-and-so, where he'd been—and I was for the first time in my life specifically asked to parties, which was very gratifying, but also a little bit intimidating. I never knew when I went to a party what I might be asked, or how to respond depending on who else was around whom I might not want to know my secrets.

Some saw me merely as a spiritual person; one who did was the wife of one of the Theology teachers, a woman whom no one else liked. We spoke together fondly of India at the faculty parties, and at her house parties she fed me hummus and chapatis and other resonant delectables. I came to have an understanding of her and a respect for her that no one else appeared to have.

Others saw me as a kind of guru or entertainment, which was a little hard to take. There were those who told everybody they knew—the Campus Minister was one of these—and that was very intimidating, for I did not trust the public at large not to come by with the scissors or a rope. I still lived in fear of the spectres of my childhood and the past.

Things got very out of control. I began to feel like a dog-and-pony show, the unpaid entertainment, for my inner sense said not to refuse to give information, which is free to all. But I resented the pushing, as I had resented helping the bullies and the podlings with their schoolwork when they were otherwise rotten to me. I guess I doubted the sincerity of some of the people. . .with good reason, as it later happened.

The Campus Minister was one of these. Slick and cool and as friendly as a used-car salesman or game-show host, he stuck himself to me with a mouthful of grinning teeth at every dinner or party, begged to hear more about his (or my) past lives, etc. He even invited us once to his mother's house for a Christmas party because he wanted me to "read" the ghosts there. His decrepit aunties who lived in the room across the hall saw things, and one psychic had already been there (for pay) to "read" the room, and he wanted to see how my information (how *I*, since he was unable to differentiate between It, Them, and me) compared.

I was rather pregnant at the time, and the last thing I wanted to do was go trudging up and down stairs in the middle of a party full of people from The Prep telling him what I saw (as if he was really paying attention, anyway). My creative energies when I'm pregnant are always directed toward the life force of the child, as they should be, and I spend very little time writing or painting or "seeing." Channeling is certainly a strain. In a houseful of potentially hostile people it is overwhelming. Hence my reluctance. But he would have been petulant had I said "no," so I did it. And came back downstairs for the last time to the party again with a frightful migraine headache and mightily resentful of him. (I still have not learned to say no easily.) He was one of the first people from The Prep to verbally burn me in effigy when I came to Virginia. "She was just a nut, a charlatan, after all." Thanks for the vote of confidence.

> *Lesson two: Mind who you tell. Be discerning in your revelations. Use your inner knowing and higher sight before you open your mouth.*

So I began to close down, to keep my dearest secrets to myself. I would give people information, just what they asked, and not volunteer anything beyond it. I became as the Four of Pentacles in the Tarot, the Miser, hording all my treasures, sharing only with a few close friends all the gems I had collected, or recollected.

Ebenezer Scrooge was not so pinch-fisted as I. Micawber and

Fagan not so niggardly of soul. The Light began to fade away. I felt desperate and trapped in the grey, mundane world, unable to find my way back to Faery; was as drear as the stark-eyed Podlings in the Dark Crystal, who'd had their essence sucked out. It was a slow, living death, and I collapsed into it, losing weight, becoming a harridan, a show of my true self. All I wanted was to escape.

Irene and company, the Gang in the Green Room, my friends upstairs, dear entity-mates, are the ones who urged me to let the cat permanently out of the bag. For some time, I had been bidden to tell the truth. Tell, tell, tell the truth about the biggest secret of my life. But I was terrified of losing what little respectability I had left, and certainly my credibility in the scholarly community. I was proud of my scholarship and didn't want it counted off to crackpot notions.

Lesson three: There are two forces in the universe, Love and Fear, and Fear masquerades as many things. Including pride. Don't be proud.

Chapter Eight

།

A Winter's Tale; or, The Long and Winding Road

I came to confront my fears after I had written Patty Jefferson's story, as a biographical novel, telling it like it was. With the best of scholarship, often uncanny to the people in the research department at Monticello, utilizing all the skills I had gleaned in my college days and in sleuthing out validations of Molly, Lelia, and others in writing their stories, I put together a work which was as true to memory, as true to the 18th century as I could make it. But it would not sell. Historical fiction is dead, I was told (meanwhile reading huge new volumes of the life of Mary Queen of Scots and Henry VIII). It's too long (1,000 manuscript pages). You are unknown. You should start with short stories, work your way up to long fiction. (When have I ever done anything the conventional way? Besides, I hate writing short stories. Too much like television.)

Cathleen had been telling me for months to send the manuscript to Virginia, Thomas Jefferson being a subject especially dear to the hearts of Virginians. St. Thomas of Albemarle. Her guides had been telling her to tell me so, and she got tired of being nagged by them. I finally got tired to being nagged by her. Being enough discouraged with trying in California and New York, I finally did it. I sent the manuscript home to Jefferson country.

This rival to *War and Peace* an extremely indulgent editor read in one week, then wrote me saying how true to life it was, but that Jefferson's career was treated as a background annoyance. . .and weren't those intimate scenes a little too much to be believed? How do we know they talked to each other that way? Why don't you cut them?

I was aghast. The intimate knowledge I had of Thomas and Patty was the whole point of the book. My back was up against the wall. I remember sitting in the library staring out the window at the trees visible through the high window. It was a clear, lovely summer day. And I was freezing cold with dread and the strong message from Irene and Thomas: *Tell the truth!!!*

Carmina Burana was running through my veins. Mozart's Requiem Mass. The 1812 Overture. Wagner's Ring Cycle. All at once.

Heart racing, I thought: If I don't say it now, I never will. And as little as I wished to be thought a crackpot, re-experience the rejection and persecution of my youth, how much more did my soul cry out to say, This is the way it was; here is the truth, and it was beautiful.

The scenes of the life were before my eyes: their meeting, all the joyous birth days, all the sorrowful death days, their world turned upside down by war, her pathetic illness and his tender regard. The final moments, when he fain would have died too, so great was their love. They cried out to me to give them voice in truth as well as in deed.

That poignant beauty, that clear view of the past, I and no other had experience of, and I alone could tell—even as I had been urged to do. I in my moment of passionate affirmation believed was worth all the scorn I might endure for the telling. Like Socrates, I would rather die for this defense than live for the other kind. Passion Mode is like that.

So I yielded. With a cosmic *yes,* and smiles from my friends upstairs, I risked my entire reputation for the sake of Love and wrote back instantly, saying basically, I know 'cause I was there.

The secret was out.

To the world, it might not seem like much. Who cared if I told some editor in Virginia that I *knew* I was Martha Wayles Jefferson in a "past" life? Was it going to be broadcast on CNN? No. So what was the big deal? The big deal was in *my* taking my courage in hand, and facing my fear of rejection squarely, and saying what I knew to be true to a person "unknown" to me (and I laugh as I write that now!), an authority figure, representing the establishment (and he would laugh at that!). The big deal was that as far as my reality was concerned, I had blown my cover forever. There was no going back.

My Journey of Awakening had begun. I had thought that I was awake before. But Realization—in the sense of coming into your own, doing what you came to do—happens in stages, as all the Masters know. You are not given it all in one breathtaking moment, though it seems so at the time of the first, even the second, Enlightenment. I certainly was not given the details of what would follow after. I could see the end product, but not the path of purification.

With good reason. As with karmic relationships with other people, if you walk into the future fully conscious of all that is likely to transpire, your basic human response is to stay right where you are, where everything is safe and familiar. (Or run in the other direction as fast as possible.) You may have the life of the devil, but it is a devil you know. It's all the unknown devils you have to fear, all that uncharted water, unmapped land. There might be lions and tigers and bears out there. Oh my. Then too, there might be paradise. You'll never know if you don't go on the hero-journey.

> *Lesson four: Follow your promptings; you will know when it is right to tell, and whom. You may not be graced with seeing fully why, but that will come clear in time. Usually very quickly. Be of good courage. They can't burn you for your visions any more. Don't live in fear.*

Contrary to Walt Disney, and more like the folktales of old, I have not lived happily ever after. I have not won the lottery, ridden off to the magic castle with Prince Charming, or otherwise found myself the subject of an episode of *Lifestyles of the Rich and Famous.* I have since endured some of the most stringent trials of my life. I thought, after my youth's experience, I could handle it. I, like the Fool in the Tarot, naively thought all would be easy and well in my journey here, ignoring the older lesson of world mythologies, and so came down hard when faced with the purification process.

That process was like being a toddler on the beach, hit from behind by a big wave; just when you've struggled to your feet, angry and shaken, another one comes and knocks you down again. . .because you're facing the shore and not the sea.

It began, ironically, on Epiphany—6 January, 1993. I at this time was full of cushy good feelings from the Christmas holidays (being a sentimental sot, with children to boot) and the recent passing of my patron saint's day (the 4th). I had my family and friends around me, and the year promised fine. I was due to travel to Monticello for the celebrations of Jefferson's 250th birthday anniversary in April (on the 7th). My son Cian was starting kindergarten in the autumn. I was looking forward to spending some time alone during the day with my daughter Ceridwen, as we had never had "alone time" before, with two older brothers. My costuming work and midwifery practice looked headed for prosperity and increase. Spiritually, I was growing and opening all the time. I would be thirty in March, outliving my natural mother. My marriage was not exactly in the best of shape, but I could live with it. Plenty of people did. Ours had never been a terribly romantic relationship anyway, and who expected romance *ad infinitum*? I would be grateful for a little space in which to Become.

I got a telephone call from a friend of mine in Virginia—Frank DeMarco, my editor—which changed all that, changed my life forever. How little of the above has transpired, remained the same! I sit here now, in Williamsburg, in the midst of a life in which nothing—utterly nothing—remains the same, least of all me.

What he said was, "We have a lot of East Coast psychics calling us with predictions of an earthquake in California before May. What do you think?"

All my Christmas cheer melted away like a San Francisco snowfall. Stunned, I stared at the sheep on my Christmas tree, which stood on the table beside me, the words resonating like harp strings. I had had dreams of such disasters ten years before. I stood rooted in fear, looking about the room, at my little house, at the cherished collected material goods of mine: my harp, my spinning wheel, my Highland broadsword. Gone. They would be all gone. How much did they mean to me, except in the memories they held of other times? My little Ceri, who was then not quite three, came into the room. Sweet Ceridwen, with her mass of auburn curls and lisp. *Mother of God. My babies!* I knew when. *I knew when!*

I said as much. April. The eighth. The day after I left to go to Virginia for a week for the celebrations of Jefferson's birthday.

I had never read about such things. I am not a joiner of groups or subscriber to "New Age" newspapers or magazines. But it correlated with what others whose life work is such watches said, as I later read in articles sent to me by my friend.

Mother of God. The trip had been planned, the date set for two years. This was Thomas' birthday, and I had been invited to be there on the mountain. Yet I wished my children, my little family, safe. What if it did happen when I was away? I could not live with myself. What if I cancelled the trip because it was expected, wanting to remain with my family in such a time of grave danger—and nothing happened? I will have missed the once-in-a-lifetime special day of the man whose life I had once shared.

What should I do? I had no wish to run around like Chicken Little. The safety of my little family was my paramount concern. We had been through one large earthquake already, in 1989, and I knew our flat to be in poor shape, never having been repaired. The most likely scenario was the top flat caving in on ours. If I cancelled the Virginia trip, I could spend the time outdoors with the children, which was no guarantee of safety, but ameliorating. If nothing happened they would just be outings with Mom. If I did not cancel the trip, I had to think of some way to keep them safe. Finally, I conceived of asking Kevin to take the children up to Lake Tahoe to visit my aunt and uncle while I was away. It would be the Easter holidays, so both he and Rudraigh would be out of school, and Kurt and Deb were always asking us when we were next coming to visit. If nothing happened, then they will have had a nice little holiday while Mom was away.

What I saw in the April dates were possibilities in the Infinite Field of possibilities. What my reaction allowed was a "reason," the catalyst, for the self-transformation necessary to accomplish what I had set out to do in this life. Nothing more, nothing less. But on a material level things were not that easy.

Kevin was rather nonplussed at the news to begin with, not being one to hold much faith in predictions of California sinking into the sea, but he wanted me to cancel my trip to Virginia. He was not keen on it on principle, thinking it a major extravagance and self-indulgence on my part. When I would not, it cleft a chasm between us that was the beginning of realization of what is so euphemistically referred to as "irreconcilable differences."

It was, to our marriage, the iceberg that struck the *Titanic*: the ship was in trouble before it ever left the yard at Belfast, before it ever sailed from Cobh, began to cross the Atlantic. It might have survived the stress of the journey, even with the inherent structural weakness and insufficient number of lifeboats, had it not been for the Captain's mad determination to steam ahead in the black waters of the North Atlantic, to "make good time." All the passengers might have survived the collision had there been an adequate number of lifeboats, but these had been eschewed; might have survived if a nearby ship had responded to the distress signal. There had even been early warnings, from engineers, from passengers who had premonitions not to sail. Instead, passengers, Captain, crew, and the bonny "unsinkable" ship went needlessly down in the cold, dark, and treacherous waters of the unforgiving North Atlantic. "All for the want of a nail. . ."

Our structural weakness was a profound lack of meaningful communication. *How we REALLY felt about things*, a mistake I don't intend to repeat again, even if it means having rows. I was always too afraid of scenes, of criticism and rejection, for honest communication with him.

We did have rows then. The first real get-it-all-out-in-the-open ones we'd ever had. (And I saw, for the first time, Paddy and Molly's—my and David's—battles as *healthy*.) We discovered how profoundly different were our world-views, how similar our desires for each other. "I don't want to keep you from being the person you are. I just want to be who I am, and not feel that you think I'm stupid (or crazy)."

I saw the kind of world we as a planet seem to be heading toward, of brotherhood and simplicity, away from materiality and, as Walt Whitman said, "the mania of owning things." I saw the kind of healing work I could do, living simply, as self-sufficiently as possible, with the earth. I had seen that sort of life for myself while yet in single digits' age. I had collected the FoxFire books and other do-it-yourself, old-timey works. As you have seen, I re-acquired many old accomplishments. I wanted that kind of life for myself, for my family. This time seemed ripe. And there was still so much of Virginia unspoiled, in which to settle. I wanted my children to know clean air, home-grown food, simple, joyous living, not be overtaken by the monster television and a crowd of useless objects. Kevin is a teacher. He could teach anywhere. I wanted my little family to be safe, and healthy. I proposed to him us all going out to Virginia for TJ's birthday. If all these earth changes happened, we'd be safe and have a new place to start. If not, it was a nice little holiday. He said no.

Virginia was not for him. He belonged in San Francisco and could never live anywhere else. His plan had never been to be just a teacher, but a teacher at St. Ignatius. He couldn't teach anywhere else.

I had used the words "Kevin hates Virginia" to people before, and they may seem a little strong. But there is a resonance operating in our relationship which puts this into perspective. The Kansas life.

It did not begin in Kansas, but for me—then Eleanor—in what is now West Virginia, in a tiny village in the mountains. A new schoolteacher came when Ellie was fifteen, a man from Baltimore with a chequered past, though we didn't know it. Stephen Markham (as we knew him) had, as James Stephens, been thrown out of West Point for drunkenness. He was actually schizophrenic. He never had any intention of settling in Virginia. It was on his way to the mining country of the West, California or Oregon, and the open freedom of the Plains. He was mad about Walt Whitman, and used to go about mumbling his poetry to himself (or shouting it). He cut a wide swath in our little corner of the world, the upshot of which is Ellie and Stephen were married. Two years (and two and a half babies) later he could not bear the confinement of our valley any longer, so decided we would go out West. Ellie didn't have anything to say about it. It was either go with him or lose the father of her children and the man she loved (but feared).

One of the children died on the way, and by the time they got to Quinter, Kansas, Ellie was so great with child that she refused to go farther. Winter was coming on. Stephen caved in and built a soddy [earthen house] seven miles from town. In the next two months, she hardly saw him. She stayed in town, awaiting the birth of her child. He was off with the Indians, being initiated by their shaman and getting ready to marry his daughter, all unbeknownst to Ellie. He unceremoniously moved her from town to the soddy, and she had her child there.

He was not around much in the next year. He would come back every couple of weeks or so, terrorize her and the children, and be off again. Ellie knew not where, nor cared. All she wanted was to go back to Virginia. Stephen, meanwhile, was undergoing profound spiritual advancement, changes, in being initiated by the medicine man. It was his hero journey, for they recognised his holiness in his speaking with the wind (quoting Whitman and talking to "himself"). He had at last found his place, the freedom for which he had yearned, searched. But he could not let go of the bond with Ellie, and he blamed her for tying him to Virginia, to Kansas, with a family. It was a relationship of extreme ambivalence. Then in the spring of 1861 Ellie had another child. And the war started.

Being an ex-Cavalry Lieutenant at West Point, Stephen lit off and joined up. His regiment was the 13th Virginia Cavalry under A.P. Hill. Ellie never saw him again. He did write twice, before he was killed at Sharpsburg (Antietam, to you Yankees), and they were the most lucid, normal-sounding letters from a loving husband at the front. In 1865 Ellie and her remaining children, three little girls, died. Afraid to move into town thanks to his abuse (thinking herself unfit for human company), she and her children were the victims of fire set by the Pawnees. And if you don't think a sod house can burn, let me tell you: it does!

These were the resonances operating. Why I felt such a strong pull to "go home" to Virginia, to "rescue" my children (two of whom had been there in Kansas), why Kevin was so adamant against going there. When I went in April, I went alone with my children. If nothing earth-shattering happened, Kevin would come and get them at the end of the month. Officially, we were separated. It was "let's see where this goes from here."

My friend who had called me on Epiphany had also facilitated my working with a woman on the Eastern Shore, setting up a holistic healing centre. Healing being a major occupation of mine, both materially and psychically, I took on this service with a big *yes.*

Kevin says when he met her at the end of April (nothing worth really mentioning having happened in the West in the way of earthquakes) he got a bad feeling about the situation, but was afraid to put too much effort to dissuading me. I would "do what I wanted to, follow my own promptings." The human part of me, that which abhors change, wishes he had! On a material level, this woman was going through some pretty tough times and just could not deal with my being there. On a nonmaterial (real) level, she was helping me fulfill my path of self-transformation and transcendence. The history books would say that, after barely a month on the Shore, I found myself out in the cold rather unceremoniously.

Where was all my Buddhistic calm now? I wanted to die. I was wild, desperate, and hysterically rang up Frank (who lived seventy miles away) from a neighbour's house. He came in the rain to fetch me, offered to store my belongings, any help I needed. But it was small consolation. I was adrift in the world. It had been hard enough on the Shore, as I had literally not been alone in twelve years. I missed my children, my family, Cathleen, my nice little quiet, well-ordered life where I was taken care of. Now I had no job, no place to live, and my small store of money was fast running out, for the bridge toll from the Shore was twenty dollars, and I had meetings down in Williamsburg (a hundred miles away), trying to get a job with Colonial Williamsburg.

But I lost more than money on the Shore. For, as I did not immediately wire to Kevin "send lawyers, guns, and money," he assumed that I wanted to stay in Virginia no matter what, and as he—in his own words—had to get on with his life, I was informed that he was beginning divorce proceedings. I was completely devastated. Our separation agreement was not two months old. The ink was hardly dry on the paper. As imperfect as our relationship was, I did not want a divorce.

To be fair to him, he wrote to me before this, saying, "I would take you back now, in spite of everything." I know now how he meant it sincerely, that he was willing to give it another go despite the fact, as he said, that everybody there thought he was a fool for doing so, when I had left him and our children. In effect it was a declaration of love, for it would mean to him considerable loss of face in the eyes of those he loved and respected. But at the time it did not sound to me like unconditional acceptance. It sounded like, "If you be good [i.e. 'normal'] from now on, you can come home." *I was afraid to say yes!* Afraid to go back to an existence of being pointed to and sneered at by everyone I had thought were my friends. My old bugaboos. For Kevin and me, more miscommunication. Our structural weakness. Such is the way marriages end.

I did not fight anything in the divorce. If he was determined on it, for the sake of the children I wanted things as amicable as possible. I had no will to fight him anyway. Warrior or no, my goal is acceptance. Some people I know do not understand this lack of toughness on my part. They think I'm the weeny woman being screwed. Our society is so used to nasty divorces with everyone fighting for years on end over teaspoons. Kevin and I are friends. Whatever might have been, whatever we let through misunderstanding slip away, is moot. We *have* a relationship with one another, as loving friends, as parents, and always will. We are just not married anymore.

For a time, I was a gypsy, a tinker, a rover. I stayed in motels, slept on friends' floors. No home to go to meant no responsibilities either. I could merely exist for a little while. I could emotionally weather this storm. But this accepting attitude would not have been possible had I not had a recollection whilst yet on the Eastern Shore. As I tightened the straps of my cartop carrier in the pouring rain, I found myself standing in the rain likewise in England, sometime in the late Middle Ages by the dress, a slender brown-haired middle-aged man in a peaked woolen cap and pea green smock. A tinker, he was hitching up the horse-harness to his caravan wherein waited a wife and three small children. "I've done this before," I thought, "and survived. I can do this." I was overcome with such peace and joy that I burst out singing,

> *I'm a freeborn man of the Traveling People*
> *Got no place to go, with No Man's Star I've wandered*
> *Country lanes and by-ways were always my ways*
> *I never fancied being cumbered*

I'm sure the neighbours thought I was a nut, but I didn't care. It helped me retain my sanity in the midst of a very difficult situation, kept me here when I would otherwise as lief driven off the Bridge-Tunnel into Chesapeake Bay.

Because I am not yet Realized, this surety did not last. One after another, fears came up and had to be faced, solutions found. Once I had a place to live, the next major panic was a job (and eating and paying my bills). I was desperately thin, and my bank account was reaching the minimum point. Nothing was forthcoming with Colonial Williamsburg (it being, as many institutions, a lumbering beast, exceedingly slow moving), and what little money I brought in doing readings for people I felt was unethically had. As with my first Virginia experience, had it not been for kindly friends, I would have starved. Learning to accept such offerings—charity according to my enculturation—was another lesson. And it came very hard.

Sometimes, it seemed that everything that could possibly go wrong was going wrong, from car problems to affairs of the heart to visiting my children. "I've done this before and survived. I can do this" became a mantra. Many's the time I would catalogue all the trials I had undergone in this and other lifetimes. "I lived through that and am here to tell about it. I can live through this." I thought often on Scarlett O'Hara, standing in the ruined garden at Tara, and her "as God is my witness" speech.

The trouble was, I still had the notion that the *I* that is my current personality was running the show, rather than my higher self. (Which, incidentally, has very little care for the trials of this plane, from a practical standpoint. Just so long as the lessons are learned, almost anything goes.)

Continually, I thought "It can't get any worse than this," and continually it got worse, until I lost all hope, all belief in what brought me here, all desire for the future. I caved in to the truth that I did not run things. I yielded to the admonition that had been tendered me for weeks by my friends upstairs: "Surrender." Layers of pride and ego were at last stripped away, not by joy, as I had refused to learn by illumination through psychedelic experience, but by trial, by sorrow. No one preordained it, ordered it, "for my own good." The universe holds no such beings. It was my own refusal to learn through joy which necessitated getting the message across to myself in this painful way. We are our own judges and juries, our own harsh critics. The loving beings with whom we share the universe—having "been there" themselves—have no wish for us to endure such pain. They wish us only Peace, Openness, Joy.

I lay in bed one night in the darkness, which was as much that of my soul as literal, feeling beaten, betrayed, and utterly alone. I saw all of my bright light and visions of love and oneness, the universe taking care of us all as the most encompassing maya, illusion. I knew

I was physically in very bad shape, and determined to finish the process circumstances had begun and quietly slip away. It would be a small thing; a couple of days without water, and pfft! I regretted the responsibility it would lay on my roommates, to inform my family. I regretted more still physically leaving my children, but truly felt that I could be of more help to them discarnate than 3,000 miles away. I was tired. Like many's the Warrior, I've had too many lifetimes too close together, too crammed with *experience*. I wanted only the peace of death. I wanted to sit in the Green Room, quaff a beer with the Gang, put my feet up, and vegetate for about a million years. I said to Irene and the rest: Do whatever you will. I don't care. If I wake up tomorrow, fine, if not, fine. I admit it: I don't run things.

Immediately, things began to change. As in, the very next morning. Jobs came, at Colonial Williamsburg and elsewhere, and messages from dear friends—Cathleen, Wendy, Cameron, and always Frank—of love and support. I was not alone, bereft. I really did only have to reach out my hand, and my heart, and feel the love all around me, embrace it. I was grateful for the work, service as it is, and even more for the affirmation from people I loved that I was not unlovable, anathema, weird. Well, maybe I was weird but it was OK. I was loved and cherished, *accepted* (there's that word again!) just as I was. This was the most important thing, for I was emotionally scarred from the divorce and from a relationship here in which acceptance of who I am was not the most notable feature.

This is how important this goal is to me; that, at this stage of my whole experience, I would have chosen to opt out for its lack. All the trials I had put myself through were to learn, *really learn* this one thing: you are as you are, make no apologies. Live in joy. As you likewise serenely let others be the way they are without judgment. All is truly well, if your focus is not egocentric. Or, as Thaddeus Golas put it, "The hardest step to take on the spiritual path is allowing people to be stupid. Fortunately, the opportunity to take that step is all around us every day."

Slowly, I regained my faith. I began to talk to my guides again, have faith in the reality of what I heard, laugh a little, enjoy what life had to offer in small, everyday ways.

It was like the healing that occurs in the grief process after a death. Except the death in this case was mine, and a way of being that no longer was viable, if I were to enact what I had come here in this life to do.

Now, the universe still throws me a curve ball now and again, just to make sure I'm paying attention, and I notice that while I still can and do get upset, my reaction is much less wild than it would have been a year ago. Not to sound like a '70s encounter group ("bad things happen to good people"), I have learned that how you experience what occurs in your life really is all in your outlook. I can take the failure of my car's battery for days on end in sub-zero temperatures as the worst thing that's ever happened to me (and subsequently be hysterical), or as an opportunity to enjoy, well-bundled, the woods behind my house as I walk to work, or the companionship of the friend who offers me a ride. "Nothing to get hung about," as the Fab Four sang. I expect that in a while I shall have attained the Buddhistic serenity I long for. . .in twenty or thirty years, for I'm stubborn and a slow learner. But I'll get there.

Do not let my little tale deter you from speaking your truth and following your vision. There is a great purpose in such trials. For in them I have undertaken the final purification of my soul. They have been my boot camp, my personal hero's journey through the Underworld. I have climbed from the Inferno, to the Purgatorio, to the Paradisio. I know my worth, my strength, and my weaknesses fully. I have, as Joyce wrote, "forged within the smithy of my soul the uncreated conscience of my race."

I am Gilgamesh, Odysseus, Beowulf, Roland, Percival, Gawain. All the way down through the ages of mankind to our modern mythic hero, Luke Skywalker. Name me a hero (or heroine), and I am he (or she). So are you. We all are.

The purpose of a hero journey is to rediscover Truth for one's culture, to embody it, and to bring it back for the culture to make use of, to help them make sense of life, the universe, and everything. We each take this journey at the end of our sojourn on this plane. It is preparation for the teaching work of the next plane of reality. It is inculcation of all the experiences we have had on this plane, taking the seeming mishmash of lifetimes, impressions, and philosophies and moulding them into a cohesive whole. It is a larger form of the soul's life review after death in any given lifetime. When integration has taken place, we move on to the next thing. Not by passing the test, by measuring up to arbitrary standards of something or someone "out there," but by experiencing it to our own satisfaction.

And the crux of this experience is truth, seeing what is, has been, as it truly is, and calling it so. Saying, "This is the way I believed. This was my reality."

Which brings us back to telling it like it is right now. Whatever your experience of reality is, it is. Know that there will be those who want or need to hear it for their own growth, for your experience in teaching, and for just the sheer joy of sharing the same reality.

Now I tell whomever the spirit moves me to tell, however farfetched it may seem to the "logical" (fearful) part of my mind, and I allow whomever I know to tell whomever they will, figuring that I'm not in charge here, and things happen as they are meant to, even if I can't always see that clearly when they first happen.

> *Lesson five: There is no wrong way to experience this plane, this beautiful little planet. Wherever you are in your beingness, there will be souls willing and needing to share the experience with you, be you Muslim or Christian, atheist or pagan.*

The point is to learn together, to love; yes, even to hate. To be here, experiencing life in all its diversity. It is the eternal play. In telling it like it is for you, you play your part.

> *And now it begins to shine*
> *And you find the eyes to see*
> *Each little drop*
> *The dawn of every day*
> *The closer I get into that open door*
> *I've gotta be sure*
> *If that's what it takes*
> *And now that it's shining through*
> *And you can see all this world*
> *Don't let it stop*
> *Never fade away*

> "That's What it Takes"
> —George Harrison

Chapter Nine

ॐ

Living in the Material World; or, Be Here Now

Having seen something of the difficulties those who live in both worlds encounter as we try to wend our way through this one, it would be easy to throw up your hands and say, "Impossible! People who see things differently can't survive and be happy in this materialistic world. They are always going to be oppressed, depressed, and generally have things made difficult for them. Well, I want to be happy! Is that so bad? I'd rather go live in a cave in Tibet."

I will admit that there have been many times in my life, particularly as things have begun to accelerate, that I have wanted to find a cave in Tibet (were it not for the current Chinese occupation) or a cabin in the woods "of clay and wattles made."

But I recognize even in such moments that a vacation life is not possible now, there being much for me to accomplish. So what's a poor member of Pugsley's Anonymous to do? How do you keep yourself from despair of this world? How do you stay happy in it, sane, when you would much prefer the Otherworld to this?

When I am feeling impatient or overwhelmed, my friends upstairs in the Green Room like to remind me of Yeats' poem, "That the Night Come":

> *She lived in storm and strife,*
> *Her soul knew such desire for what proud death might*
> *bring*
> *That it could not endure the common good of life*
> *But lived as 'twere a king*

> *That packed his marriage day with banneret and trum-*
> pet
> *And the outrageous cannon*
> *To bundle time away*
> *That the night come*

And it does remind me that I am here to integrate the two worlds, to live in this one in full consciousness, and to teach what I can to whomever comes to learn, before I can go off to my next lifetime, my vacation in Iceland. So I begin to lose some of my impatience with people who cannot or will not see as I see, and I recognize again that they are not being deliberately obtuse merely to annoy or thwart me.

I remember Thaddeus Golas' words about letting people be stupid. This is not intended as an insult, but to help us remember that there is not *one way*, but many Paths on the road to Enlightenment, and that I/you/we were once where he/she/they are, and that things are perfect just as they are. But when one is filled with the zeal of an enlightening experience, to let people be where they are, not to try to change their minds, get them where you are, is hard indeed. What to do?

Be. It is that simple.

Be as you are, and let others be as they are. If it annoys you to see them as they are, "missing so much," then turn on your "other vision" and see them as they will be in a little while, realized, glowing, beautiful.

This works! With the belligerent, with the fanatical, with the depressed, with the pathetic, with all those who are struggling. It helps also to turn your vision on yourself, and remember when you were as they. This is the source of true compassion, which differs markedly from pity; not "there but for the grace of God go I," but "there go I." For so-and-so and you (or I) really are the same. It is only the convention of this plane of reality which leads us to think that we are separate creatures.

So, be. If you feel the urge to teach, to get the message out, rest assured that the "students" will come to you! For in so being as you truly are, the light you cast upon the world will shine out to them like a beacon illuminating their way.

The basis of this beingness is, of course, Love. It has been said by many teachers throughout the millennia that there are only two forces in the universe: Love and Fear. Fear is the more seductive, likes to masquerade itself as Rationalism, Reality, Common Sense.

But Love is the stronger and more powerful, and will ultimately prevail.

Any action taken in fear, no matter how carefully one's ego might construct it to look like common sense or rationalism, is bound to fail, for it by its very nature is negative. The negative energy congests itself, binds together like a tumour, and blocks the positive force of love. And, unfortunately, until we progress beyond this plane, we are all subject to it.

What is called for here is Roto Rooter, Drano for the soul. And when one is clogged up with the materiality of this world, perhaps frustrated that nothing seems to be going right, that one is unappreciated by the podlings of this earth, what is required is indeed a little "out time," a reconnection with the Divine. That cave in Tibet sure begins to look good! But most of us can't accomplish that, or even time to meditate our way out of our clog. So we become depressed, or ill, or suffer from eating disorders or migraine headaches. Anything to escape.

Well, help is available! Painlessly. It doesn't cost much, or anything at all (and you won't be questioned at the border by the Chinese). And you don't have to give up your "real" life responsibilities to avail of it.

The simplest thing I know to do is to walk, out in nature. Spending a good half-hour a day outdoors, reconnecting with earth and sky and stars and Other seems to be a minimum for me. You will find your own level of need, which will probably vary according to what's going on in your life.

Living as I do in Tidewater Virginia, there are woods everywhere at a very short distance, which is nice for me, as I love the woods. But the riverside is also close, and—at a little distance—the broad Atlantic.

Now, some of you may be saying, that's as well for you, but I live in the city and there's nowhere within fifty miles to go. It's all concrete and it's driving me nuts. I don't have a summer cabin. What am I to do?

When I lived in San Francisco there were community parks everywhere. Up the corner from our house was a ranger station where the Golden Gate Park police boarded their horses, and this was a favourite spot of mine.

Every city has parks. Avail of them. Don't mind if you have to share the park with children, strollers, and dogs. In fact, sharing the space with them is reconnecting in itself. Sit or lie in the grass—or the sand, if there is no grass; don't mind the looks you get for playing in the sandbox with no kid—under a tree, or not if there aren't any. The point is, be with something natural. We get very clogged up easily in our modern world with its concrete and plastic.

Sit, or lie. Breathe slowly. You do not have to close your eyes to put yourself "elsewhere." In fact, it's best not to, as that puts you inside your own head, which can be a noisy place. The idea here is not to get into yourself, but back into the universe (which is of course, in yourself, but I mean not roiled up in your own trip; this is not psychoanalysis).

Feel the grass, or sand. Feel the trees. Feel the sky, the stars, and all the beings about you which may have become unseen in the harriedness of everyday life. Feel their vibration. Open yourself to it. I guarantee that inside ten minutes you'll be beaming, seeing every screaming child at the park, every derelict lying on a bench as a being of perfect light, filled with love and beauty.

One of the other ordinary things one can do is go to the movies, or pop in a video at home. But be specific as to the movie you watch. *Rambo* is not going to do it here. The movie ought to be something that speaks to you, whether by virtue of its historical period (revisiting old haunts) or its essential message.

Immerse yourself in the action, the drama. Put aside all concerns of believability ("the willing suspension of disbelief"). I.e: Don't be critical! Accept what is before you in its own reality. Experience it fully. Pamper yourself while so doing. Eat popcorn, and gooey movie snacks. Or, if you're at home and so inclined, have a glass of wine and a bit of cheese and crackers or fresh-baked bread. If it is an historical piece, indulge in period snacks. Mead or ale with Errol and Olivia in *The Adventures of Robin Hood*; sherry with Basil and Nigel in *Sherlock Holmes*. Whatever. You get the idea.

As to historical films, your own taste and inclination will direct you to what feels comfortable (predicated on where you've been before), so I can't really give you a list suited to a general public. Besides, your inclinations will have much to do with what is resonating in your life at the moment.

Sometimes I feel like watching *Forever Amber*, and sometimes I feel like *Spartacus,* or *The Egyptian,* or *The Lion in Winter*. Go with the flow of your feelings. If you're feeling ratty you might just want to indulge in a powerful, moving story. For instance, if I were feeling put upon, I might choose *A Man For All Seasons* to give vent to my funk rather than *The Great Race* to jolly myself out of it.

Sometimes, sitting down to a movie is not what you want or need either. Sometimes, what's called for is a little mood music. For those of us who are compulsively busy, music is often the best relief from disconnection and ratty feelings while we accomplish those things we "need" to do on this plane. The inventors of Muzak know very well how background music can affect people's moods, much to the delight of grocery and department store owners, who have benefitted monetarily from it.

When I'm feeling disconnected I sometimes like music that is a real blast from the past: Tibetan or Gregorian chant (both of which are guaranteed to drive family and housemates crazy); Indian ragas; Celtic folk and traditional; early or baroque instrumental; romantic or classical piano; ragtime and jazz. But other times, there's nothing like a good pop song to get me back into what's real. If this seems a little farfetched, lend an ear to the words of one of George Harrison's songs:

> *Precious words drift away from their meaning*
> *And the sun melts the chill from our lives*
> *Helping us all to remember what we came here for*
> *This is love*
> *This is la la la la love. . .*
> *Little things that will change you forever*
> *May appear from way out of the blue*
> *Making fools of everybody who don't understand*
> *This is love. . .*
>
> *Since our problems of being are our own creation*
> *They also can be overcome*
> *When we use the power provided free to everyone*
> *This is love. . .*

There are many pop singers or groups whose music carries a message, not necessarily as consciously as George's always has, though those from the 1960s and '70s certainly did. Those remain my favourites, and how lucky that their popularity has circled around again, and they are more readily available. I was laughed at for years for liking John Denver's music, but now the tenets he espoused are kitchen wisdom: universal love, ecology, childlike joy in life, a different way of seeing. There's some vindication in that, and the lesson that if you wait around long enough, mankind is bound to catch up with you sooner or later.

One of the problems associated with seeing both sides of the world is that there is no one world religion or philosophy which encompasses everything one understands and is free of culture-specific identification. Some religions come pretty close to the universal truth common to all religions; Taoism, for instance. But even with that, you have to have an innate acceptance of the culture from which the religion sprang for it to feel right, and if you're harbouring lingering resentments from some far past against the culture (having been murdered by Mongol hordes, say), all the "rightness" of the philosophy is likely to go right past you. This goes for that Western favourite, Christianity, too.

The answer seems to lie in taking in everything and distilling from it what feels right and ignoring the rest. This is not calculated to make you popular with fundamentalists, but you probably aren't anyway, if you've opened your mouth at all in front of them, so relax and gather your gems of wisdom where they lie. The fundamentalists will come 'round when they're ready.

This open approach can lead to some fairly peculiar experiences. Cathleen and I went one Sunday to a procession and Festival of India in Golden Gate Park. This had been a yearly occasion since the Summer of Love—1967—and was sponsored by the Hare Krishnas. Never having had any experience of them beyond watching them on Haight Street and at airports, I decided that this would be the perfect opportunity for exploration. I had no intention of becoming a Hare Krishna. I had—and have—no intention of aligning myself with any particular religion any more in this life. I simply came to experience and to indulge in some nostalgia for India.

It was a glorious summer's day, and I threw myself into the procession with joyful abandon, being completely in the experience, dancing and chanting with the rest as we pulled the cart along the five or seven miles through the park, giving over every reservation I had ever been enculturated into about these people, and found. . .not a moment, but a long day of pure joy and connection. It was one time I knew right well there were hordes of people looking and gossiping, thinking I and the rest were complete wackos, and it didn't matter. I loved those people who criticized, as I loved the people in the procession. I loved Cathleen beside me (who had been my sister-in-law in India), saw her as she was then, and laughed in sympathy at her current complaints of "firewalking" and toasted feet (as she had left her shoes in my car). All was open and joyous and free. There is certainly truth in everything, and it is up to us as individuals to find and cherish it, without judgment.

This view of non-judgment was tested several times that day, from many angles. Once was in watching the rudeness or politeness of people as we waited in the long lines in the meadow for the food, which was provided free (a world-wide service of the International Society for Krishna Consciousness). To see the grace and patience— or lack of same—with which the multitudes acted was extremely enlightening: I could tell at a glance who was a follower and who was not; who amongst the followers had truth and love in their hearts, and to whom it was merely a platform. My heart ached for the ones not yet "there." They were in such needless pain, fruitlessly searching for something which was to be had in a heartbeat, within themselves. I wanted to take their hands and say, "Be happy, brothers." I perceived why the Hare Krishnas give people flowers. My feeling was not the pity of the superiorly-minded, thinking "Oh you poor sod, I have *it* and you don't. . ." I have been, can be still, in times of depression (the last neurosis left the Old Soul), where they were. Compassion is not pity. It is love to the umpth degree.

Another time was at the "cow protection booth," which advocated vegetarianism as one of the cures for the world's hunger. A tourist was badgering the lovely young devotee, who bore all his spleen with equanimity. Gentle and gracious, with her love she made even the man's wife question his ire. The devotee never criticized the tourist's choice to eat meat. Her method was gentle, uncritical enlightenment—information—endeavouring to persuade the man, by reason, logic (to which he could relate), and love, the cost in money, acreage, and ecology that meat manufacture had for the planet, for those living now, and for unborn generations. The tourist finally walked away in disgust, unable to tear down what he saw as the girl's pose of loving acceptance, which we espied was his true motive. He wanted the Hare Krishna girl to abandon the teachings of her faith and upbraid him, doubtless so he could say the whole religion was a crock as he had thought all along. But he could not tear down Love. Nor did the girl, once he was gone, complain of him, though there were several people standing about (not devotees) who did. She only shook her head sadly and expressed the hope that he would someday be more open to other ways of being than his own.

Lesson three came to me directly. "Now," my friends upstairs were saying, "you have been in a state of grace all day. Test it."

Cathleen and I were standing talking to the author of a little book of aphorisms, about philosophy, beliefs, karma, and judgment. We spoke in agreement of the yearning to be free of this plane, to dwell unencumbered, having achieved nirvana. The author looked at me directly and averred that to be free from earthly entanglements all one had to do was chant "Hare Krishna" (which I had been doing all day) a certain number of times.

Cathleen stepped back and turned away from us at this, knowing well my mind, my knowing, and my temperament, which has not been generally inclined to suffer fools gladly. To her astonishment, I did not blast the man with forty-seven reasons why he was misled and misleading others with such a pronouncement. I merely nodded and wished him well in his endeavour, bade him "namaiste," and we concluded our conversation.

Asked to explain this astonishing reaction, I could only say, "He wouldn't hear what I had to say; it would only alienate him. He'll come to know what's true when he's dead or progressed. I'm not going to beat my head against the wall trying to convince him now." Besides, he may be right.

The point, which I well understood from my guides, was that wherever everyone is is OK. There is no wrong way to be, no need to preach or scorn, or self-deprecate, either. Truth has many faces, many guises, each as valid as the other.

One of Kevin's students was at our house one day, looking at my "religion" bookshelves, which encompassed everything from the Maryknoll Missal to the Bhagavad Gita and Book of Pagan Rituals. She looked from it to me and asked in bewilderment, "So. . .what are you?"

I might have given her a smart answer, or an evasive one, saying that my anthropological training led me to collect works on world religion, but instead, I gave her the truth: "Everything, and nothing."

This answer is rather psychedelic, to which state of being this student could relate, and begs the question of drug use to "get you there." Having recalled many experiences through the millennia of ingesting various psychoactive substances, I am hardly in a position to cast stones, and even in this life I am not without experience of aids to transcendence, from humble nutmeg to LSD. But I prefer non-chemical means, such as meditation. This is not due to any moral outrage, as I figure these things were given to us to experience and are inherently neither good nor bad.

Personally, I don't see the point (except escape) of drugs such as cocaine that don't trigger a mind-altering experience. Psychoactive substances do have their use in "getting you there," and can be a quick shortcut to profound revelations of the nature of beingness, but sooner or later you find other, more permanent means of transcendence. Such as meditation.

Two anecdotes come to mind in relation to the use of psychedelics:

In 1967 Baba Ram Dass, then Richard Alpert, fresh from his experience at Harvard with Timothy Leary, went to India with a load of LSD to see what the yogis thought of it. He had become dissatisfied with the limitations of the drug-induced experience, and knew that India had a long tradition of spiritual awareness that closely paralleled his psychedelic revelations. He gave large doses to many yogis, who were unimpressed, including one who took several doses of 600-900 micrograms (which should have sent him flying through the roof!). This holy man simply sat, unmoved as before, and when Baba exclaimed in astonishment at his fortitude, said with a wry twinkle in his eye: "This is good. But meditation is better."

Then there is the remark of George Harrison's regarding the Beatles' famed use of acid: "LSD did unlock something for me, released all this stuff. I used to spend time looking at myself in the mirror and the face kept changing, from looking like a Mongolian and then to a Chinese man. I just kept looking, thinking 'Who *are* you?' I think that with pot it did something to the old ears, like suddenly I could hear more subtle things in the sound. But now I've found it's actually better not to do it while working. I need to be a bit more clear because my mind is such a scramble at times, and all that does is scramble it more." [*Musician Magazine*, May 1992]

But once you "turn on," you never forget it. The insights that come in that state are never forgotten because they are outside of the realm of perceived time. For this same reason, you can re-experience it anytime. Even lifetimes later, as happened to me upon recollection of a brief sojourn in the hometown of the Fab Four.

My incarnation as Richard (Dick) Bunton was in direct reaction to the previous lifetime in Poland during the Second World War. Having endured a miserable childhood in a Jewish ghetto and an early death at Birkenau, I had a strong desire to cut loose, to experience the sensuality of life, as did so many survivors of the war. So I hopped back into life in 1944 as a beatnik artist, a Teddy Boy, in Liverpool, hardly before the soap made from my Polish boy's ashes was cold enough to be used.

Dick was an artistic soul, and the post-war conditions in working-class Liverpool were hardly conducive to fulfillment of hedonistic desires. The desire to paint—especially experimental, avant-garde paintings—was ridiculed by the provincially narrow-minded folks who made up his world, and as he grew up he became increasingly frustrated with the restrictions and limitations of the time and place.

He started off decently enough in "adult" life, at fourteen, by working at the docks. (He was tall and lied about his age.) He never did get his leaving cert (British equivalent of a diploma) but it didn't matter to him. "Art doesn't require it," he thought. But he fought mum and dad about it, who naturally wanted their only son to be reasonably educated. This early independence and free contact with the outside world did him no good. Sensitive to trends, and craving experience and acceptance, he hid his true nature in the pose of a tough and wore leather and tight black jeans or the outrageous pseudo-Edwardian garb of the Teds [the Mods of their generation]. He discovered the beat scene and clubs like the Casbah and the "dark, damp, and smelly" Cavern. He still painted, still privately sought a more expanded way of being, but it became as much a tweak of the nose of the establishment as a true artistic endeavour.

It was the club scene that became his downfall, for in addition to being a place to hang out and meet birds [girls], it was also a place to make drug contacts. And make them he did. Pot was all right, in his opinion, but its mellowing effect interfered with his artistic output, so he gave it up for the thrills of the then-drug-of-choice: cocaine, or cocaine-and-heroin. At some point, he became a dealer of both these substances. By the age of seventeen, he had an enlarged heart from the drug use and suffered a series of minor coronaries. He finally died of a heart attack after OD'ing one early November night in 1961. He had been to The Cavern that night with his girl, Anne, watching a local band play.

I had always had a fascination with the beat scene and the Fab Four; one of my very favourite early childhood dolls (I do not recall how it was come by) was a beatnik chick who said hip things when you pulled her string; I had an instant love of the San Francisco coffeehouse culture; and a very early and strong anti-drug stance (in middle school I looked down with secret disgust at the potheads and trippers in my class, although, as they were among the few people who accepted me, it remained secret). But I never put it all together. I thought it all an aberration, or at best a memory of the astral when I was casting about in the '50s for prospective parents. I was wrong, as I discovered one night recently.

It was the tolling bell of the combination of club-scene-and-drug-use that woke me up to Dick's experience. When River Phoenix died, I was positively obsessed for about a week with the details of his life and death. I thought I must be losing my marbles, as I hardly knew who the kid was. Yeah, he played the young Indiana Jones. Oh cool, he was a vegetarian, isn't that nice? Yawn. So why in blazes was I suddenly obsessed with his experience in and outside of the Viper Room? I didn't have an answer. But my insatiable fascination continued.

Then I was sitting with my friend Mary in her car after a dinner out, and she was talking about her emergence into consciousness in the '60s, and how much the Beatles had to do with it (as they did in so many people's lives), and suddenly I found myself—a tall, thin, rather scruffy young man; the sort of person my grandfather means when he refers to "the masses of the great unwashed"—standing in a cold sweat at a table in a dark, noisy, smoky club, very high and knowing something was desperately wrong, trying to focus on something to keep from freaking out. He chose the guitar player in the corner under the concrete archway. He had a familiar, comforting sort of face that didn't change into something weird and freaky at will. The young man was Dick, and he had taken his lethal dose. In that moment, I knew everything about him: we were in England in the very early '60s; the girl sitting before him was Anne, his girlfriend; he lived in a bungalow with his mum and dad not too far away; he ostensibly worked on the docks. . .His whole history and short future was before me in a flash.

The observer part of me, Kelly watching this, looked at "the guitar player in the corner" too, and was zapped with a shock of recognition: *My God, it's George!* "Somewhere in England" was specifically Liverpool, November 1961. The club was The Cavern, and the "local band" was the Beatles. Dick was about to go vomit in the loo, take his girl home, and collapse with a fatal heart attack in the kitchen of his parents' home in the small hours of the morning. Everything made sense: my fascination with River Phoenix and my fascination with the early Beatles, who were well on their path by the time I—Kelly—hit the scene in '63. I grabbed Mary and exclaimed, "It all makes sense!"

Then I had to explain what I meant. An hour later, when the story was out, the shock had still not worn off. I called Cathleen, I called Kevin, I called Frank, for a reality check, all with the shocked news, "I was a beatnik drug addict in Liverpool!" The responses were typical of the individuals: Kevin asked how long I had felt the resonances (why it hadn't come up before); Frank wanted to know how I knew; and Cathleen, bless her, replied casually, "Oh yes, the Teddy Boys. . .Cocaine was the drug of choice then." Not a word among them of "you scuzzy lowlife layabout," which was my reaction. *I WAS A DRUG ADDICT!* It was horrifying.

My enculturation said drug use, let alone abuse, was moral depravity of the worst sort, even though "everybody did it." Never mind that I could blithely accept my use of hashish in Crete and India. That was religious. I was afflicted with guilt and remembered with a great sense of shame my disgust of college friends who used cocaine. What a hypocrite I was!

I asked myself why this had come up now in my life. Was it merely a caution against excess in new-found freedom? That seemed unnecessary, given that I am essentially too domestic and too Otherly focused to cut too loose. It seemed too puritanical for my "there is no black or white, right or wrong, you can do what you want, no experience is any better or worse than any other" philosophy. In that philosophy lay the reason. *Apply it to yourself!* Irene and the Gang said. And I did. In meditation. In that soul-searching application, I discovered that what was called for here was self-acceptance on a very deep level, real knowing that in spite of past or current actions which I find reprehensible, I am still a part of All-That-Is, loved, valued, necessary, accepted. Yes, drugs can "get you there," but, as the yogi said, meditation is better.

I have a great compassion for that part of myself that was Dick Bunton. It was a hastily chosen lifetime, but not unwise. For had I gone directly from the fire of Poland, it would have been too easy to be holier-than-thou because I had innocently endured so much abuse and degradation, too easy to feel that the world owed me something by way of retribution. But there was Dick, with his craving for life experience, his joyful abandon, hedonism. From a holier-than-thou perspective, it would be easy to see his life as seventeen wasted years, yet from that poor strung-out desperately seeking artist came the lesson that we are all, while on this plane, subject to its lures and passions, and there's nothing wrong with that. From Dick's experience has come love, self-acceptance, and balance. Coming to terms with Dick's life and drug use has made me peaceful, with the sort of peace that has the potential to last.

In the scientific literature, there is a phenomenon known as recurrence or "flashbacks." It is common to have spontaneous flashes of the psychoactive state for up to eighteen months after a single use, as the drugs create a neural pathway pattern which facilitate the release of serotonin in the brain. Brian Wells, in his *Psychedelic Drugs,* cites one psychologist who could spontaneously re-experience the psychedelic state *ten years* after a single use of

LSD. Remembering, feeling Dick's state of being as he stood in front of the table at The Cavern has made me wonder if there is not a psychic version of recurrence as well, since the same neural impulses cause flashbacks of both past-life memory and the psychoactive state. I have had experience of recurrence in this lifetime already, was familiar with it when I saw Dick, and I believe that it has much to do with the way I am.

It has been said that psychoactive drugs cannot change one's philosophy—cannot make a spiritual person out of one who was formerly not, and that the nature of the experience (whether transcendental, consciousness-expanding, holy, or "a really satanic bummer") is largely predicated on where you are in yourself when you take it, and who you're with. So there's something to be said for my being weird from the start and for my first hapless experience with psychedelics being merely the boost over the top.

Once in an altered state, I had the weirdest feeling of physical *deja vu*—coppery taste in the mouth, a spinning sensation in the body, to say nothing of altered perceptions of sense stimuli (hearing tastes, etc)—and stilled my mind with the thought: I've had this experience before in this life. *When?* Searching back through time, I stopped at a picture of myself at the age of seven, eating breakfast cereal. *It was in the cereal!* A relatively small amount of LSD, put there by my then brother-in-law, who was living with us. Regardless of the ethics of this action, its most profound effect was that *no one noticed anything weird or different about my behaviour!* Which should say something about the way I was generally. I don't blame him for what he did, for in the long run he facilitated my beingness. (Which is not the same as saying I am okay with the possibility of someone doing it to my children. You'd see the broadsword out then, by thunder. If my children want to experience psychedelics later as adults making a free choice, that's one thing—and their business— but they are not adults now and such an action against them would be seriously bad karma. Happily, I know who they hang out with while not with Kevin, and the possibility of such an occurrence is slim to nil.)

One of the reasons I'm so blasé about mind-altering substances is that I can remember so many lifetimes of experience of them, when it was not a sign of moral decrepitude to make use of them. It's hard to be indignant when you've got a few million years rattling round in your head, full of everything from mushrooms and hashish to Scotch broom.

In his book *Food of the Gods*, Terence McKenna puts forth the thesis that psychoactive substances, namely psilocybin in the form of mushrooms, were responsible for man's "ascent" into consciousness. The chain of events being that psilocybin induces an expanded state of awareness (God-consciousness), which requires words to express its effect on the spirit. It also affects (enhances) the neural pathways for speech, making such communication possible. This information was very persuasive, for it rang a dim bell in my head, back to the days in East Africa, hunting and gathering, pre-"Lucy" (about 3 million years). With it came recollections of other times of drug use, which, as I've said, I blithely accepted:

In Europe at the end of the last Ice age, there was broom, heather, and an alpine plant which defies modern identification in my mind but which was low and had little white flowers like gowan.

Then there was Egypt and Sumeria and Crete, the whole ancient world, where mead and other wines laced with hashish and cannabis-smoking were part of religious ceremony. The same is true for India and the Far East, and the use of henbane and opium.

The excesses of the Romans are well-known, and as a soldier I was not without experience of cantharides, and, had not a bash in the skull killed me, I likely would have died from it or venereal disease eventually.

In Europe as a monk in the Middle Ages there was belladonna, broom, and mugwort used in Church rituals (albeit, unsanctioned).

In Ireland and Scotland we had the same. It was these highly abortifacient drugs that Margaret MacLeod used and Lelia Larkin prescribed.

In Virginia in the 18th and 19th centuries there was laudanum, which was used in my experience as a painkiller in childbirth, and a doorway through time.

In Ireland, Molly used it to dull the pain of tuberculosis, and "visit" Mick in America.

And then there is Dicky. It was utterly terrifying and infuriating when he realized he'd OD'ed and was about to die. He was a firm nihilist, and felt he'd really blown it. "Wait! Wait! I haven't *done* anything yet!" (I would like to point out here, for those who might not know, that cocaine is *not* a psychoactive substance.)

So with this long, mostly religious use of drugs I can hardly condemn their use in these days of "Just Say No." They have a respectable spiritual history which is not likely to be eradicated even with paper-shredders and book-burners abounding. Even if all written evidence disappeared tomorrow and the whole world got amnesia, mankind would eventually "rediscover" psychedelics and make use of them, for in the ego-dissolution of the experience there is peace and a sense of interconnectedness with all things, which our souls constantly seek. Intrinsic faith that such oneness exists, despite our personality and society's negative override, is what keeps us all going. Essence *knows* the truth of our beingness, and speaks to us, through all our doubts and fears.

Faith is often a dirty word these days. In some circles it implies you are a sort of cosmic chump, or a Pollyanna at the very least. But the most important thing to do when faced with obstacles—human or material—and circumstances which seem to contradict the reality that you as one who lives in an expanded reality know to be true is to have faith.

Know that you are not crazy.

Know that you are not wrong.

Know that your vision, formed in love and forged in truth, is sure.

Know that at every moment there are literally hundreds of unseen friends—guides, entity mates—about you, lending their support, their love, and their visions when you feel you have lost yours.

Remember the Christian story of the man who at the end of his life saw it as footprints in the sand. He noted two sets of footprints most times, and only one at others. He enquired of Jesus why this was so, as he recalled that the latter were the hardest times of his life. He asked, "Why, Lord, did you abandon me?" And Jesus replied with loving compassion, "I did not abandon you; those were the times I carried you in my arms."

So it is, however you want to call the powers that be.

Finally, rely on your earth-bound friends who love you and share your vision. Lean on them. They will support you, as you support each other. This is most important. It is practice for the reality beyond where we no longer perceive ourselves as separate beings. Love means accepting aid as well as giving it. We are all one together, as the outrageous and beautiful Freddy Mercury of Queen wrote:

> *One man, One goal, One mission*
> *One heart, One soul*
> *One flesh, one bone, one true religion*
> *One voice, one hope, one real decision*
>   *Give me your hand, give me your heart*
> *Cause I'm ready; there's only one direction*
> *One world, and one nation*
> *Yeah, one vision*
> *No hate, no fight, just excitation*

All through the night it's a celebration
Yeah, one. . .vision.

The guys in the Green Room say "Amen to that!"

Chapter Ten

Guru; or, Man on a Mountain

Having opted out of the cave in Tibet in favour of hanging out in the Western world, you may have thought you avoided the pitfall of the Tibetan cave: seekers after knowledge coming to you, O hermit monk, for your pearls of wisdom (for plainly, if you made it there, you must have all the answers). Well, lemme tell ya, it ain't so.

There are seekers everywhere who, for various reasons, would rather have you tell them the truth (or, some of it, anyway) than go out and find it for themselves.

Some of these are earnestly following the path to enlightenment, and these people will come to realize, as you have with your own teachers, that the path lies inward, and no one can travel that road but you. (As Glinda said to Scarecrow in *The Wizard of Oz*, when he asked why she'd not told Dorothy that she'd always had the power to go back home to Kansas: "She had to learn it for herself.") Such "students" will have their time with you, and then—if you are not invested in ego—seek their own ways. Some will remain good friends, become teachers themselves of you and others; some you will not see again in this life. If you let things flow and view the whole of existence as a continuum, this can be quite pleasant for everybody.

Then there are the sycophants. Otherwise known as leeches, court fops, or the cosmically bored. They're the ones who run after every new fad of enlightenment, desperately seeking Susan, without any real intention of getting anywhere. They're running on a treadmill, and you happen to be on currently between *Geraldo* and *Regis & Kathie Lee*. They want instant and easy answers: They'll meet Mr. or Ms. Right, win the lottery, and move to the Bahamas; they are last-lifetime old souls and can do whatever they want because it's their vacation; in various past lives they were Aristotle, Marc Antony (Caesar's death is too messy), Francis Drake, Napoleon, *and* Louis Pasteur. They are the first to praise, the first to tell all their friends about you; also the first to call you a fake because you *won't* give them easy answers or you show some evidence of humanity. And they are first to build the bonfire. Joan of Arc should have such friends.

But show a little kindness to these last. After all, they did trouble to seek you out and such persistence deserves some reward. Remark on their diligence, don't be judgmental, and give them the all-purpose answer (courtesy of *The Restaurant At The End Of The Universe*): 42. It's guaranteed to perplex them, send them away thinking deep thoughts, and allow you to eat your pita with tomato and sprouts in peace. What if the answer to their question is not 42? Well, somewhere in the universe, at some time, they will have a question the answer to which is 42; and since all time is now, consider their question as properly answered and get on with your lunch.

Levity aside, what does one do when faced with a roomful—or a constant flow—of people who look to you for the answers to mankind's great questions? (Karmically speaking, should they wear the purple nail polish with the rose lipstick?) Golly gorsh, it's enough to send one of Pugsley's Anonymous beating a hasty retreat to the local kiddie sandbox, wondering How Did This Happen To Me, and What Am I Doing Here; I Don't Know Nothin'!

First, we might look at some of the ways we get ourselves into teaching mode, and you can feel where you fit into the scheme.

There are those Christ-like souls—such as Billy Graham, Mary Baker Eddy, and your high school chemistry teacher—who consciously know their mission from the outset and pursue it diligently and with dedication. This is rare, even with very old souls. Personally speaking, I didn't have a conscious urge to teach until relatively late, and even then it was more in the next category than this one of peaceful acceptance. No way did I want to be stoned for itinerant preaching.

The second path, the way it came to me and very many others, was the Knock-You-Over-The-Head Path. Otherwise known as The Case of Mistaken Identity, or The Life of Brian. Think of the members! Buddha, Gandhi, St. Paul, Einstein, Ramtha (aka Judith Knight), and Shirley MacLaine. Not one started off in life by rolling over in the cradle and saying, "I'm on a mission from God." Each had some incident that turned on the light for the teaching mode. All had led more or less ordinary lives, even if they did seem a little out of sync with the rest of the world. But there was no burning urge to broadcast their weirdness via the airwaves. And when the call first came to teach, the reaction was "Who Me? You must mean someone else!" Acceptance of the path came only after much prompting, to put it mildly, from God, or their guides, or All That Is. To those beings of higher vibration, getting so-and-so into teaching must have seemed like pushing a kicking mule uphill in the mud! My own guides have been preternaturally patient with me, stubborn Warrior that I am.

The third teaching way is related to the first in terms of acceptance, for these teachers never consciously realize that they are in a teaching mode. They are so focused on service and the everyday manner of their service that it never occurs to them that they are a candle in the darkness to anybody. They just blithely do what they do, and are grateful and happy to do it. This group includes people like your postal carrier, the man at the nursery who can coax any plant into abundance, and Mother Theresa. No amount of praise will sway these gentle people from their essential humility and simplicity, and therefore they make the best teachers. They would blush at being called teachers and would say they are in no way worthy, being too human. In short, they would not believe you. But you remember them forever.

Modesty being a commendable virtue, there has been through the ages many the entrepreneur posing as a self-effacing teacher, only to be exposed as a fraud when it becomes clear that the motivating factor of the teaching is money, and not the true desire to aid mankind. Therefore, as teachers, whether we come into it willingly or not, we must constantly ask ourselves whether we are truly humble—realizing how much we are only slices of life and not the whole pie—or are merely putting on a modest show as that's what's expected. It's the old saw my grandmother used to quote from her childhood in the 1910s and '20s: "You're not the only pebble on the beach." Any time teachers begin to think they have all the answers, you know it is no longer open teaching, fluid and connected, but dogma, whose concern is control rather than liberation.

Personally, I find the whole idea of putting on a show of any kind, be it of modesty or of channeling when I'm not, completely repulsive. The day I start doing that is the day I dig a hole and pull it in after me. There seems to be a literally universal standard for true teaching against which to measure oneself, and I am ever acutely

135

conscious of it, as I would hope anyone who is drawn to teaching would be, no matter their emphasis.

I have asked myself many times since I consciously accepted this teaching role, how did I get here, and why are these people coming to *me* for answers? When looked on for wise counsel, I often get a very Brianesque (as in *Life Of*) feeling of panic that they have the wrong woman here.

For when looked at on the face of matters, it's absurd: I am younger than most of the people coming to me—or at least they are my peers. Why should they believe that I "have it" and they don't? Yes, I have garnered a very great deal of experience in this lifetime already and remember considerably more from many past ones; and yes, I do have a "tap," if you will, into unseen realms, but the information is only as good as the receiver on any given day, and I do have my own biases, or editing, which undoubtedly sometimes influence the material, particularly if I'm tired, or if I have some emotional interest in the subject at hand.

With all these caveats running constantly through my head, it's quite difficult to get a swelled head about being the great wise teacher, the Hermit, lighting the way. I might aspire to that, but I'm certainly not there yet! So it makes me extremely nervous if people tell me how wonderful I am. Wise friends of mine on both sides of the veil call this a case of self-deprecation, and perhaps it is so. But I know my own humanity, my faults, very well indeed, and I don't want to be the source of someone's disappointment for being "only human after all," after they have built up an image of me as some kind of sainted being in their minds.

My first instinct after such a remark is made is always denial, and some elucidation on my plain ole humanity. But I have found this to be ineffective—for it is often thought to be false modesty—and sometimes downright counterproductive. The sycophants especially can get hostile if you try to burst their bubble about your state of enlightenment.

This seems to be part of their process, that is, seeing you first as the saviour, then as basely human. Hopefully sometime down the line they will come to the correct and balanced view that you know something, and can help, but are still here on this plane too for a reason; but meantime, it's best just to be patient, say thank you with sincere humility, and leave the rest to the powers that be.

When you come far enough along in your path, you really do realize how much you are an infant in this vast universe, that this plane and its little play is only the kindergarten for what lies beyond, and that realization can be very daunting. How can you teach when you don't know nothin'?

Simple: realize that, though you are a kindergartener, you are a graduating kindergartener, ready for first grade, and fully versed in the mysteries of how make and peel mint-flavoured paste "skin"; what the best items are for show-and-tell; and what the rules and regs are for naptime. . .and realize that the incoming class need to know these! It might not be much, but it's more than they've got at the moment. So it is with passing on your enlightenment. Know that it *will* be helpful to *somebody,* however imperfect it may seem to you.

So there you are, having found yourself sitting under a tree like the Buddha or perhaps more prosaically in a coffeehouse with some acquaintances or friends, and they ask you—almost but not quite rhetorically—since you seem to have it together, what you think of life, the universe, and everything; or they desire your opinion in how they should progress in certain matters. At any rate, *voila,* you find yourself teaching, quite unforeseen and unintended, but you're doing it.

Word leaks out. You gather in greater numbers at the park or coffeehouse. Soon, this arena becomes too public for so many people; you retire to your house—or someone's house—for your sessions. The numbers here too grow, and perhaps the number of nights in the week you spend talking of unseen matters.

People call you on the phone between times. They call you at work. The focus of your life is no longer your straight job, if you have one, and your own progress, but the lives and concerns of those who are coming to you.

You begin to feel like the teaching is taking over; you have no private life etc, etc. You begin to have a real empathy for Christ and Gandhi, and your local shepherd, surrounded by clamouring multitudes. All you want is a little silence, a little peace, a little time to play.

"Calgon, take me away" crosses your lips with greater and greater frequency, with less and less humour. This is known as burnout, and can lead to moments of real empathy with less savoury people, like Son of Sam and the McDonald's murderer.

Then there's guilt, especially if you're Catholic or of one of the missionary Protestant sects. No matter how stressed-out you are, you feel a responsibility to those who come to you. Be they sincere students or sycophants, you cannot bail out on them, much as you might want to.

The choice appears to be heading toward going down for the third time yourself or blowing your credibility. You ask yourself, How did others deal with this? Christ (Buddha, Mohammed, Krishna, Gandhi, whomever—most of them, —Realized Beings or not— ended up dead, and anyway you decide you're not in that league. So where does that leave you? Packing your bags for the nearest rubber room?

Hopefully, not. Though packing your bags is a good idea for a start. Like for the mountains, or the desert, or wherever is nearest by for you. Take several days off. Go camping, or simply rent a cabin (a motel room being a little too removed from nature, generally). Get away from the phone. If you have one of those newfangled handy-dandy car phones that is usable within a hundred miles of your number, ditch it.

Believe it: all those who "depend" on you will be there, more or less as they were when you left, when you return. They might be a little put out that you "deserted" them for your own "selfish" purposes, but if they are truly mature and on the path, they will think no such thing, if you explain gently that you just need a little time to recharge. Even the Energizer Bunny needs to be plugged in once in a while.

This is also a good way to weed out the sincere from the hangers-on, as the court fops will find some other entertainment in your absence. And that will leave you with the sicnere seekers.

While you are away from home, do nothing, or as close to nothing as your ethic will allow you, for at least the first day. Go on a fast if you wish. Sleep. Lie around and stare at dust motes. You remember doing that. It's how you first found your friends on the other side. Do nothing for as long as you possibly can, and when you can stand doing nothing not a moment longer, do nothing some more. This is known as "non-action." Also as Couch Potato (though TV is obviously a no-no).

And when you've gotten through the itchiness of doing nothing and it is truly comfortable again (and if this sounds like the process in meditation it's because it is), pick up the one book you have brought along with you. This can be something spiritual or philosophical or escapist. But really get into it.

Examine the words, as words. Take their sounds apart. Look at them and repeat them until they don't mean anything anymore and you can't remember how to pronounce them. You remember doing this as a kid, don't you? Or maybe during some drug experience you had in your misspent youth? (If this sounds like the process of using a mantra it's because it is.)

When you've done with that, and you really begin to question your perceptions of any reality, *then* sit back and look at your life, teaching, and relationships, and ask yourself and guides what right action is; you'll get a much clearer answer than you would have gotten when you were ready to send your loving fellow beings on a one-way trip into the Otherworld. You'll be able to sort out who and what is truly important to your life, and how much you need time to play or merely vegetate.

After three or four days—or a week or two, if things at home were that bad (and we would hope you'd not let them get that bad before a sense of self-preservation kicks in; that was Survival 101 back on the Serengeti Plain)—you'll be ready to go back, a plan in mind, if not in hand, the Serene One once more.

This is a process which will probably recur several times as you change levels in your progress and teaching. Don't be dismayed if it does. Don't be dismayed either if, as you progress, you find your student level dropping steadily to a core of half-a-dozen or so, or whatever, as the goats are weeded out from the sheep.

This does not mean that there's something awry with your teaching. What it does mean is that those who are ready to make their permanent exuent from this little stage are relatively few as compared to the mass of humanity.

Personally, it means you've stopped playing to the pit, or even to the gallery, and have gotten yourself into a master seminar on Technique For the Actor, where all the names are illustrious ones, and all the people who go with them are there because of their dedication to their craft. There is no greasepaint here, there is no ego. This is the place where theory and practice meet, and it is Reality. The scenes played out here, and the discussion of technique, the finely tuned and loving critiques will be some of the most sublime moments you will experience on this plane. And most of it will be completely spontaneous, written on the wind.

This can induce in the susceptible a sense of sadness. "If only the world could see this!" But as with the gang of men who followed a certain carpenter around, what is shared here is not meant for one and all. They would not understand it, for it is some of the most far-out information a human being will ever come across. It is the Inner Inner Circle. The place of eternal secrets that every mystical tradition guards from outsiders.

For those who would mourn the ephemeral quality of such

encounters—hardly "teaching" now, but sharing—let it be said that this is only the beginning. The whole of the astral plane is dedicated to it. That's right, just one big Encounter Group! And you thought you left Esalen behind with your bell-bottoms and polyester print shirt with the scattered cartoons of Mickey Mouse, somewhere in the mid '70s. Surprise! Did you wonder why *The Big Chill* was and is so popular? So get you ready for a couple hundred years or so of touchy-feely.

Now, for a few observations:

1. Practically speaking, regarding teaching, in spite of the answer "42" earlier espoused here, the best way to deal with sycophants or the skeptical is to treat them sincerely, as the realized beings they are in the "future." You'll take some heat from the skeptics—but aren't you used to that by now in your life? Most of what you say will go right over the sycophants' heads, but the words will be remembered, stored on the great circuit board of their eternal memory, to be recalled at some time far in the "future," when you will be but a dim memory of a time and place long past in their experience. The Tibetans have it perfectly right: treat every person as if he is Buddha. . .because he is!

2. I never have liked the idea of charging for channeled readings, and I am very uncomfortable when people offer to pay. The under-lying thought in my mind is always, "If they pay for this, even for 'my time,' then it is goods and services, and they have the right to refunds or bad feelings if their lives don't turn out the way they want." I also feel that this lovely gift I have is inherent in all beings, and therefore not subject to fees. To wax Thoreauesque, should we be taxed for the trees, for the clear air, and the warm sun? These too are mankind's inheritance. This is not likely to sit well with the thousands of people out there who earn their bread in this manner, and do so—to their minds—ethically. Of course, this is a free-will universe, and earning your living by teaching is one of the pathways; but I have come to a point in my journey where it is no longer the way. Other people are in different places, and can do what they want. I will accept barter—I don't mean an all-expenses-paid trip to the Bahamas—in something I can use, such as eggs or a winter blanket or new shingles on the doghouse, and perhaps this is a good indica-tion of where I at least am heading in the future (or the past, when hard money was a rare or nonexistent thing). You may not think barter is such a hot idea, and that's fine. To each his own.

3. Finally, coming to accept one's role as a teacher (which you chose to do before coming here again, anyway, we are reminded)

can be one of the hardest steps on the spiritual path, because of both its potential for power-tripping and its painfulness for the humble person. But, as many a monastic has learned through the millennia, excessive humility is a kind of pride, too. In Tibetan Buddhism, the seventh and final step on the path to nirvana is taking no pride in having achieved the former (very grueling) six. Christian and other monastic traditions have the same course.

I remember well when I first encountered this truth, and how the circumstances of it profoundly changed my understanding of reality.

For several years I had known about Raji, my Tibetan monk, and I accepted this with ease. I saw him very clearly in the last three years of his life at his hermitage in the Himalayas, dressed in white clothes.

After seeing an exhibit of sacred Tibetan art at the DeYoung museum in San Francisco, I was puzzled. The Dalai Lama's own monks, who were there making a sand mandala, wore cranberry and a yellow-orange; orange I had seen too, and crimson, but never anywhere did I see white. So I rang up the owner of The Tibet Shop on Polk street and naively asked what sort of a monk would wear white. Sweet George, he was very patient with stupid me: he paused briefly, and in ever-courteous Tibetan fashion said gently,

"Monk? No monk, but yogis, hermits wear white. . ."

I was stunned.

I nearly dropped the telephone, and it was all I could do to splutteringly convey my thanks for the information and make a decent farewell.

I was a yogi!!!!

The information was devastating. How could I have been a yogi—great holy man—in the 15th century and be what I am now, so imperfect? I was not led to believe that progress went into retrograde, like Mercury and Mars. How could I have been a yogi, so holy? I was not nearly enlightened enough. Shouldn't that have come at the end of my cycle of lifetimes? My monk had been an exceedingly realized man. So how come I was still stuck with impatience as a (very annoying, to me and everybody else) Chief Feature?

Then there were the manifestations. *He* did all sorts of fascinating things, the like of which you read about in *Ripley's Believe It Or Not* or see on episodes of *In Search Of.* I am nowhere at my monk's level. So I asked, What *is* going on?

The guys upstairs all said, *This was fuel for the journey, for hasn't it been a wellspring of wisdom to you thus far? And besides, what makes you think it happened "so long ago"? It's happening right now! Your view of "time" is only a convention of your particular society and not even consistent on your planet, let alone on the physical plane.*

Well, blow me down! This required an entire rethinking even of esoteric matters. Slowly then, I made a greater exploration into my monk's life, as before I had been content merely to know the outlines—saw the course of his path and why he ended up in that dark little cell which clung to the edge of the Spine of the Mother [the Himalayas] like a new-born monkey; and came to accept both that I had been what our society perceives of as a very holy man in Tibet, and that it was not in fact in the past. I accepted, but it took the jolt of a clunk on the head—very like the one delivered by the Mongol that ended Raji's life—to wake me up to it.

The realization that made this acceptance possible was that, to quote the Tibetans, "In the sacred space, every action is a mandala; every sound is Om; and we all are Buddhas." Where I am, so are others, and so shall all of us be."

So when they call you teacher, guru, and look at you with faces shining with love, or lay their heart-rending miseries at your feet and ask you to make them better, smile and accept it all with grace, for in so doing you teach the greatest lesson to those souls: where we're going and what it's all about. And that is Together. With Love.

Chapter Eleven

ॐ

Brave New World; or, The Number of the Bus

(Channeled from the Gang in the Green Room)

Bright star reading this, having traversed many pathways from your separation from the Infinite Being, of which all are a part, having suffered much, endured many sorrows and exulted in many joys, it is well that you stop and ponder, come at last to the end of your sojourn on the physical plane, where indeed you have been, where are going, and what lies ahead for the planet on which you have spent so much, as you perceive it, time.

It may perhaps not have escaped your notice that in the last fifty years particularly of your historical time there has been an acceleration of events, both of a material, physical nature, and of a spiritual dimension also. To those of you who are so inclined to look at the cycles of history, and see corollaries to other time-space realities, we commend your thoughtfulness and insight. To those of you whose eyes are just being opened to the possibilities of realities, we assure you that such upheavals are for the infinite soul a mere blink of an eye, and not to mire yourself in fear of losing either your life—for indeed in any real sense as we perceive it this is impossible—or your little planet's habitability. Rest assured that it will continue as it has done for much longer than your current science will allow for, although breakthroughs are being made in terms of knowledge which will shortly upset the scientific apple cart in that respect, and will overturn the current paradigm. We speak here primarily of news from Egypt, which we will discuss in greater detail presently.

Our channel, she whom you know of as the physical author of

this book, is here somewhat reluctant to pursue our current line of thought for fear of being thought entirely mad, which should come as a lesson both to her and you all that while yet incarnate on the physical plane, no matter the high levels of love one is engaged in, there is still the opportunity for fear to make its presence felt. We encourage her and you all to forge ahead through the churning waters of your fear and accept that which comes to you from the high planes, however unreasonable it may seem when received. We remind all that such "everyday" miracles in your reality as electric lights and central heating were once also the product of direction from the high planes.

That stated, recognized, we will commence our overview of your little planet's true history with as much accuracy as a human channel will admit of. Our purpose in so doing is both to educate you as to the true nature of your physical reality, and to ease your very human fears concerning the future, for many of you have some notion of what is about to occur on your plane and are apprehensive.

It would avail us nothing to begin too much before your last planetary shift, as such reality would be so far removed from your current experience as to fall into the realm of science fiction. Yet we enjoin you, as you read this, to listen to the voice within and ask yourself whether or not the information in fact resonates. This is known as validation, the practice of which is one of the highest forms of communication on your plane, for in so doing you are literally reaching out to the stars.

On a purely physical, geological level, it has been noted by many of your scientists that the magnetic poles in your earth are at wild variance with the current polar axis, and that these bear striking relationship to geologic stratae. This is good work. However, we would advance the notion that the geologic dating methods currently used are grossly inaccurate, and do not reflect the truth of your planet's age, excepting in circumstances which are humanly impossible to be reached, as in stretches of the Alps, the Pyrenees, and the Himalayas—the latter particularly.

This noted anomaly has produced no little confusion amongst scientists and the 'rational' public, whose paradigms do not allow for the possibility of the reality we are discussing. It is most simply stated that your planet is far, far older than you have been led to believe heretofore. And that the magnetic fields in your earth reflect this great age accurately. We are saying in short that your planet's polar axis has shifted not merely once, as most of your scientists are willing to admit of, at least in a marginal degree, but many times.

The last time was approximately 5 million of your years ago, although we use this number with some caution, the reason for which we will elucidate:

Your planet was then much closer to your sun and a twin of the planet you call Venus. Thus the years as perceived of by those on your planet were shorter than currently. It is also true that your planet spun in the opposite direction. Evidence of this has been recently found in the discovery that the course of some of your major rivers was once opposite to what it is now. The physical plane reality of this is borne out by memories now surfacing of those now incarnate of the sun rising in the west and setting in the east, which has long been thought to be pure childish fantasy by the skeptical. Let us assure this was physical fact.

It is well then that you might ask what caused such a tremendous shift that would knock a planet several million miles farther into space and set its spin in an opposing direction. You have no further to look than your own moon, and the asteroid belt beyond the planet Mars.

This meteor shower was great enough, long-lasting enough to effect a major upheaval on your planet, and to cause the decimation of a primary culture, whose legend comes down to you as Atlantis. The culprit in this case was your moon, which glanced off your earth's surface, much as one billiard ball hitting another, causing a wide rift to open up undersea in the Atlantic, and the skittering out into space of your planet. Yet so strong was the gravitational pull of your earth that the moon was propelled along with it, to settle in its current circuit around your earth approximately three million years ago. We would here ask the skeptical to search their memories to see how this resonates, and not to be influenced by the constraints of your enculturated reality. There are those among you who remember both other life forms before your present species, and the disorientation of returning to a planet vastly changed after the settlement following the last shift.

We are not unaware of the ramifications of this information upon the perceptions of time and history upon your culture, and we would stress the traditions in both the near and far east which maintain this information as part of their reality.

There was afterwards, at least in terms of the physical plane vessels, a period of "starting over" which allowed for a great influx of infant souls upon the plane, whose levels of awareness required simple life styles, as much as the shift had allowed those old souls who were ready to depart your plane "excuse" to do so. For those already in the midst of their progress, the shift was a spur to growth in consciousness, and as such was chosen to be experienced.

To speak briefly on the nature of life before the last shift, we will say that the level of technology available not only met but exceeded your current Western standards, as many are aware. The question then arises in the minds of many as to why such a technologically advanced culture could not foresee, prevent such a catastrophe from occurring. To this we respond with the query to you in your late twentieth century reality: are you technologically capable of preventing the assault upon your planet of an asteroid shower? Any reasonable person would have to answer in the negative, as did many of you then.

There is the psychic component to be here considered. That is to say that the level of awareness had become such upon your planet then that the souls incarnate called the asteroid shower to the planet to experience that reality, and this is technically correct. We would add that this was enacted by the upperclassmen, if you will, the older souls upon the planet, the younger souls being so much along for the ride, willing to experience that which was enacted, but choosing not to influence the reality chosen by the older souls. The parallel to your own time-space reality should be obvious here to those in the least versed in current so called New Age thought; it has once again become apparent to those older souls on your planet that you collectively influence your physical reality, but the younger souls prefer to see themselves as victims of circumstances beyond their control. Each reality is as valid as the other for the souls experiencing them.

There have been many in the so-called New Age community who have experienced the physical plane "reasons" for the "fall" of Atlantis—which we would point out was not the name used by that culture of itself, but your language currently does not have sufficient concepts to convey the name succinctly—and we would sat that these are valid in so far as they are the physical manifestation of the true, or non-physical reality. The events which occurred then are a response to the etheric reality. Such is as true in your time as was true then, for this is one of the basic tenets of the universe, the reason for which we will illuminate:

All That Is consists of a vibrational frequency, much like a radio wave, unseen but perceptible in a certain circumstance. At very high plane levels, this vibrational frequency is extremely pure, and your language has not words to convey its purity. It may be perceived of in the mind as a blinding light, an electric current, or heavenly music, for such is the filter of the physical apparatus. For those of us off the physical plane it is beyond such concepts for we can perceive of it without physical correlation. However, even we, at our level of the mid-astral plane, recognize that we cannot perceive of It in Its true reality, our vibration being slower, denser if you will, than It's.

Pure energy, to become physical matter, passes through a process of increasing densification, from pure energy to thought, to light, to sound, and finally to particles of physical matter, which includes the physical plane. The Astral plane, at which we are, has a resonance of matter, being less dense than the physical plane, and more dense than the planes above. Thus we may create anything we want out of the available energy here, for it is extremely malleable, a fact which those perceptive old souls on your plane have discovered, and make use of with joy. As we create our reality here for our own play, much as you have begun to do with virtual, or holographic reality, so do the souls upon your plane on an essence or soul level every day. Thought creates matter. Thought creates the manifestation of "outside" events, "causes" in your physical reality. It has been said before but we will reiterate, there are no victims; all is chosen by the soul as an experience upon the physical plane.

So the Atlanteans by their essential consciousness drew to their planet the physical reality of a monumental asteroid shower, literally created the asteroids out of the stuff of the physical universe, and directed their path into the planet's sphere, specifically to experience that reality, as the time had come for a shift in consciousness, and this wanted reflection in the physical reality, much as your household surroundings, that with which you chose to decorate and furnish, reflects your interior reality.

So too, all of you on your plane are calling forth out of the stuff of the universe the physical changes manifest in, on, and around your little planet as the level of consciousness changes in response to individuals' progress on their paths.

This reality you have seen recently in the noted increase in floods, hurricanes, volcanic eruptions, wild fires, earthquakes, and other natural phenomenon, so that to some baby and young souls, these indeed look like "the last times," a biblical Armageddon. To some it will be, for there are many who are choosing to exit your plane at this time rather than to experience that which is about to occur.

We would not seek to frighten you with such words. Believe that your worst nightmares are by and large worse than that which is heralded. In the United States you have seen widespread flooding, fires, earthquakes, hurricanes, and yet the structure has not utterly collapsed. So it is within the rest of the world. As we have stated to many querants on this matter, there will be earth changes, but the greatest change will be in the hearts of the people. If it is your desire to survive through the coming times to what lies beyond you will do so if not, you will opt out.

From our perspective, that manner of change is largely immaterial, although we will say that you seem to choose the hardest way possible with alarming frequency. When will you learn there is no need to wear yourselves out so, that growth comes also from joy and not merely through pain? Yet there is a dramatic element to the proceedings we view, and that is a consideration in choice, as is the general soul age of your planet's inhabitants. The younger the soul the more drama is included in life. Older souls tend to be lazier, preferring to learn through joy, or in some cases, inertia.

We are aware that the first change which comes into your minds is the threat of a nuclear holocaust. While we would say that you are not yet entirely out of the woods in that respect—for the technology still exists—it is not the primary form of physical change on your planet. Most of you have opted, as a planet, to experience "natural" changes rather than such an "unnatural" one. Whether you experience them as individuals is, of course a matter of personal choice.

We would outline for you some of the world-wide changes we see over the next hundred years:

* The United States will have an inland sea, this being provided for by the widening of the course of the Mississippi, Missouri, and Ohio rivers.

* The Hawaiian islands will increase in size, due to volcanic activity, as will Iceland; the latter to more than double its current land mass. Generally, there will be an increase in volcanic activity world wide. Japan should expect a major eruption of Fuji, and a raising of the level of the Sea of Japan, as the volcanic activity increases underground.

* There will be a marked change in two mountain ranges as the tectonic plates shift: the first of these is the Caucasus and the second is the Himalayas. There will be noticeable changes in the Alps and the Pyrenees, but these will not be as great as in the other two. The opening up of new areas of these mountain ranges will allow for the discovery of remains of very ancient cultures on your planet.

* Egypt and the whole of North Africa will experience flooding to a degree not heretofore seen except in very ancient times, will become in fact once again the green valleys they were long ago. This will lend "scientific" credence to the newly expostulated theory that the erosion on the Sphinx at Giza was due to water, and will lead to the discover of the history of very ancient cultures, including what you call Atlantis, of which the man Cayce and others have spoken.

There has been much discussion in the "New Age" community concerning manners of living through and after these changes, and we would remind you that each will experience reality according to his own inner nature and his placement on the path.

* Many very young souls, late level Infants and Babies, will experience the "cave dwelling" that some have seen. This is due to the fact that this is all their interior structure will allow for comfortably. Technology frightens them, hence they will retreat into simplicity.

* Late level Baby and Young souls will tend to experience the highly technological, "futuristic," computers-and-spaceships reality that is exemplified in the Star Wars series of films put forth by Late Young soul George Lucas. This fulfills their need for drama, and a sense of control over their environments

* Mature souls are the most likely to experience a lifestyle of "naturally-generated" power sources—solar, water and wind powered generators, and a melding of technology and "earth-friendly" practices as it is these souls who are responsible for the current— by which we mean in the last fifty years—public awareness campaign in that arena. This is the focus of their learning and teaching in the cycle; the family of man and the responsibility each has toward that family. This is the age of humanism. If you look at the practices of Late Mature countries in your world: Sweden, Finland, Norway, Iceland, Denmark, Switzerland, to name a few, you can see these practices already well-established.

* Late Mature and Old souls are the most likely to opt out of the system entirely and make a play for living off the land, going back to simplicity, "pioneer ways," and generally engaging in what is known as self-sufficiency. This fulfills their soul desire to live in trust that all will be provided for—a ridiculous proposition to earlier cycles. It also fulfills the crotchety desire in some to be left alone.

These will become hermits, living alone miles from anywhere, who spend their days fishing for their supper and other useful endeavours while they inculcate the lessons of the physical plane. It goes without saying that the skills these souls possess and make use of are almost entirely based on far-past experience. Some of these souls will never have picked up a hunting knife or a fishing pole before, never built a house or mended a fence. They will simply go off and "know" how to do these things.

In your culture there has been much fear generated of "survivalists" in a catastrophic situation; those souls who have spent their life stockpiling foodstuffs and weapons, and who, in such an event would be ruthless against any seeker after aid moreover that bands of such renegades will roam the countryside commandeering whatever they can in the way of supplies in whatever fashion. We would say that there will be some of this. More isolated pockets of it, as cities break down as cultural centres, rather than the general rule. You have such now in your cities, except that you call them gangs. We remind all those on your plane that nothing happens to you without your consent. If you experience an encounter with survivalists, it is because you have chosen to do so.

These individuals are, by the way, most often young souls with some strong memories of the last shift and other hard times, wherein they were, by their perception, helpless. They are determined not to be so again. It is part of their cycle to insist on their way no matter what, and to otherwise create dramatic scenarios for future play possibilities. Some of you would call this karma, though as we have stated, we disagree with the victimization inherent in the popular notion of karma.

So it remains up to the individual soul what precisely they shall experience in the next few years, and how they will respond to it. There is no right way to experience the changes, there is only each individual soul's way. Rest assured there is no Judgment Day awaiting you at the end of this change, except as there has always been at the end of a lifetime, a self-review of actions and attitudes, which is ultimately loving and directed toward becoming ever-increasingly aware, open and loving.

What lies beyond the farther end of changes on your planet is not precisely, as some would have it, a return to Eden, although there are those souls who will perceive it that way, but a change in awareness of your collective place in the universe and how it fits in with the whole.

Entire new chapters of your history are about to be opened up to you, and at the same time, communications from other life forms in your solar system and beyond it will be made consciously for the first time. These are merely two sides of the same coin, that being expansion of your collective awareness. There are some who will find this new paradigm frightening, even threatening. There are others to whom it will feel very comfortable.

Neither of these reactions is right; they are merely reactions. When you step beyond reactions into the realm of secure beingness, no longer flung about from pillar to post by "unforeseen" changes and "outside" influences, when you realize that you are the cause of all that happens to you, then you will have arrived, and will have no more need to return to the physical plane. Meanwhile, the play goes on.

Chapter Twelve

ॐ

The History of Weird; or, Bill and Ted's Excellent Adventure

For those of you who feel that such weirdness as I and others exhibit is a product of the "New Age," is a modern phenomenon brought on by the stress of contemporary life, an escape or other diversion, or who labour in the small hours of the night with the fear that it's just you and no one else has ever been this way before therefore you must be certifiable, let us now embark on a short history lesson.

I can hear the yawns and see the expressions of horror crossing faces even as I write this, but rest assured that history is not a boring jumble of facts and dates, but the adventure—the life story—of fellow sojourners, as entertaining as anything George Lucas and Steven Spielberg can concoct for our current entertainment; especially in the case of the organically weird.

Since we must begin somewhere in the stream of ever-occurring consciousness (that is to say, life), let us splash into the river in a chronological manner, if only for the comfort of those who find leaping to the farther stones a bit taxing at this stage and who would prefer to traverse the river in an orderly manner.

The first of our weird friends from the so-called past is Socrates. Socrates is one of those people about whom everyone has heard and practically no one actually read, via his friend and admirer Plato. The name Socrates rings a bell, but it is distant, and we get a picture of some grey-hair sitting on a stump pontificating—or maybe, if we know a little more, sitting in a bathtub with a hemlock cocktail while his friends hang out. Some wild party there! But what did he actually do that was so outrageous, and how does he qualify as being a founding member of Pugsleys Anonymous?

He was born in Athens in 469 B.C. This is our date, which he would have found incomprehensible, for the Greeks were not at that time anticipating a Christos to appear in Judea 500 years in the future. Imagine Europeans sitting round the hearth in their towers or hovels in 900 A.D., cowering in terror of Norse raids, having a sudden flash of Columbus, Raleigh, Drake, and Magellan—and all that came back with them. Inconceivable! So it was for the Athenians concerning that humble carpenter. Most of them were too concerned with getting ahead in life and having a bit of fun to ponder imponderables. Then there was Socrates. . .

Socrates was a ne'er do well, a loafer of no profession, who simply wandered around talking to people. He had no ambitions in life beyond this, and seemed to get by well enough. His parents had been artsy-craftsy people, his father a sculptor and his mother a midwife. Doubtless, they had tried to instill in him a respect for the artisan's life, but it never took.

During a midlife crisis, he got tired of wandering aimlessly around and tried a career in the army, where he wandered around to a purpose (and some people say he joined up to get away from his wife Xanthippe, who was a real shrew, as who wouldn't be, tagging after a man who didn't care where his next meal was coming from), but the novelty of that soon wore off, and he was back to the life of a semi-nomadic philosopher.

He attracted large crowds, but not because of his personal charisma. He was fat, bald, ugly as homemade sin, went barefoot, and stood for long periods in a daze, or talked to himself about the gods and the nature of the universe. His contemporary (one can hardly say friend) Aristophanes caricatured him in his work *Clouds* and Socrates' reputation as an oddball was secured.

He was not a creative thinker, but he had great enthusiasm and was not averse to calling a spade a spade. This, in combination with his upright moral attitude, earned him many friends—the same friends who later were responsible for his being brought to trial. I grant you, he was not hanging out with tax-collectors and prostitutes, but the effect was the same on the minds of the people, for Socrates' friends were young aristocrats.

What did he do that was so offensive as to get him thrown in the pokey? To answer that, we must take a look at Greek society at that time, and what his competition was.

Most people in his day and age were happy to make their

obligatory obeisances to the gods and leave it at that, to enjoy life and not question what words and concepts like *courage* and *honour* meant. Most people did not wander about talking to themselves about man's inherent nature and his relationship to the divinities. Most people did not natter on about moral goodness or see it as their bounden duty to point out others' defects of logic and morality or poke pins in the puffed bladders of society's much-cherished beliefs.

Socrates was a profoundly moral man, spiritual, as we would say, and he admitted to hearing a supra-natural voice which directed him against wrong-doing. It was his sincere desire to help humanity, by setting forth the logic of right action and

exposing the faults of unquestioning acceptance. To do this, he developed a means of teaching which is familiar to us today: that of questioning the student as to the meaning of familiar abstractions. He was asking his adherents to look at the world for themselves; essentially, to *be in* the world they were in, to be conscious of their surroundings and the true effect of their thoughts and actions. This is a great deal to ask from people whose primary focus in life is to party till they drop.

In 399 B.C., three Athenians brought charges against Socrates for being a public menace; for heresy (his "divine voice" being viewed with great suspicion); and for corrupting the minds of the young.

In his defense, *The Apologia*, Socrates promised to set forth his case in straightforward language, more suitable to a man of his age than—as he said—the schoolboy oration of his accusers. He cited the Oracle at Delphi as the cause of all his wanderings about, questioning everything and everyone, as it had said he was the wisest of men, and he had set about to prove it wrong. He was regretful that the parents of some young men who had nothing better to do than follow him about saw him as a pestilential busybody who filled their sons' heads with wrong ideas.

When the guilty verdict and death penalty came, he was not particularly distressed, but said that he never cared for the things other people cared for; that he had no intention of minding his own business; that he was condemned because he did not grovel as they wanted; and that he would much rather die as a result of this defense than live as the result of the other sort. So he imbibed a vintage glass of Chateau de Hemlock while his friends looked on, and Plato called him a saint and wrote a quartet of pieces in honour of his teaching and everybody felt properly lousy for what they had done, which was Plato's object. All of which goes to show you that if the Oracle at Delphi says you are the wisest in Athens, accept it graciously and rest on your laurels; unless of course, you have a fancy to experience the Otherworld firsthand.

If we trip along a couple of years, we meet with a fellow by the name of William Blake, son of a London hosier, a self-confessed visionary whose radical ideas about life, the universe, and everything were as shocking to his contemporaries in the so-called Age of Reason as Socrates' were to the Greeks.

Born in Picadilly in 1757, he wrote of his early life that "Inspiration & Vision was then, & now is, & I hope will always Remain, my Element, my Eternal Dwelling place." In earthly life he saw and felt "Bright shoots of everlastingness," and these he expressed through some of the most remarkable poetry, pencil sketches, watercolours, and engravings ever to come from the pen of man, whose beauty and vision are as unfading with the passage of time as the sunset or the song of the lark.

But Blake was regarded in his time as something of a crackpot, surely as amoral, and struggled with the castigation of himself and his works by an unappreciative public. All manner of depravity was attributed to him, which reputation he probably earned, as he was fond of sitting naked in the greenhouse with his wife reciting poetry; expostulating on the wickedness of the burgeoning Industrial Revolution; and regarded kings as an unnecessary evil. He applauded the French and American revolutions, and it was widely rumoured that he kept Thomas Paine's neck from being stretched by sending him to France.

We expect such eccentricities from artists now, but not so the 18th century. And Blake's early life was anything but conventional. His father was a Baptist of Swedenborgian leanings, a devout man, who nonetheless was disturbed at his son's behaviour and his wild tales of visions.

The boy loved the woods and rambled freely about the countryside on the outskirts of London, bathing naked in the ponds. When he was four, Blake declared that he saw God's head at the window, and at eight or nine he saw a tree filled with angels. He had also seen the prophet Ezekiel under a tree in the fields. For telling such "lies," his parents thrashed him soundly, but William's visions continued. This ungovernable redhead was never sent to school, about which he wrote,

> *Thank God, I was never sent to school*
> *To be Flog'd into following the Style of a Fool.*

But he didn't miss much, for at the age of ten he was sent to a drawing school, was then apprenticed to an engraver, and after that attended the Royal Academy, where his first showing at the age of twenty-two met with mediocre success. *The Death of Earl Goodwin* is an allegorical painting concerning the death of a tyrant. All of his early historical paintings were allegorical, for he longed to express the "poetical vigour" of such scenes.

Besides, at the time he much engaged in the mob rioting of Newgate Prison, where conditions were less than posh. He detested government and was a follower of Milton. So if the blue noses at the Royal Academy did not like his art, he should hardly have found it a surprise, for Charles Dickens and the popularization of humanitarianism was fifty years in the future.

Throughout Blake's art, poetry, and life there runs a symphony of mysticism. In modern parlance, he was into the occult. One of his favourite books was Cornelius Agrippa's *Of Occult Philosophy*, which showed how "the human form divine, expresses in its proportions the power of numbers"; that "Man's body is a measure of the universe."

Blake believed that pagan wisdom expressed Christian truths and traced this thread of truth from the Magi, the Jews, and classical wisdom to his contemporary Christianity. To him, all religions were one and symbolism was universal, thus it became his primary working language.

He expressed himself in a "fourfold vision": Single vision is only that which is seen by the eye; twofold vision perceives the human value of things; threefold reveals thought in emotional form and is the impetus of creativity; and fourfold vision is mystical ecstasy. Blake saw the world, lived his life in this way, and was wounded that the pundits of the time called his work "simple." In such "simplicity," he found marvelous complexity. This was a man who would make a deep pun, then wonder why nobody laughed. It's hard to live your life on four levels when those around you perceive maybe two.

He was no ascetic in the physical sense, this passionate pilgrim, but enjoyed all earthly delights, and wrote once,

> *Abstinence sows sand all over*
> *The ruddy limbs and flaming hair,*
> *But Desire Gratified*
> *Plants fruits of life & beauty there.*

He and his engaging wife, whom he taught like a good disciple to read, write, draw, and engrave with him, never had any children except Blake's works, though he always loved children and in his youth rescued the underprivileged in Dickensian fashion.

But Blake's greatest weirdness, like that of our friend Socrates, was that he took dictation from the disembodied; more particularly, from his dead brother Robert. He channeled some of his best writing from his brother's words, and it was Robert who gave him the knowledge of a new way of copperplate engraving, the secret of which stumps experts to this day.

The relationship of the Blake brothers was Orville and Wilbur on a higher plane, both being artists whose work was synergistic. When younger brother Rob died at the age of nineteen, Blake began, as he said, conversing daily and hourly in the Spirit with his brother. It was to him, he said, a source of immortal joy that he was in this mortal life conversant with angels. He made watercolours of Robert's spirit form, and told friends of his relationship. In those days, this qualified one as a candidate for Bedlam.

Blake had conversations also with Shakespeare and Voltaire, saying that the latter spoke to him in a manner like the touch of a musical key: probably in French, but he heard it as English.

Blake's vision, and visions, saw him through all manner of life's difficulties with grace. When an admirer of his and Wordsworth's came to visit, he noted amid the squalid atmosphere—the dirt, the poor furnishings—the overriding gentility of the Blakes.

When favoured with a reading of Wordsworth's poem *Intimations of Immortality*, which the visitor had brought with him, Blake understood and best admired the parts of it that confounded its reader: the metaphysical.

He admitted to having no care for money, but his wife was frugal and thus kept Blake's soul from escaping its earthly confines too early. It was a good thing she was frugal, for when he died they had but a few shillings and no money to print up any copies of his work. But he left no debts, a testament perhaps to his wife's skill.

Before he died, those watching said his countenance brightened and he burst out singing of the glories he saw in heaven. They counted him as having died a saint's death, with which Blake would doubtless have agreed, for once when asked what he thought of Jesus Christ, he declared that, "He is the only true God. . .but then, so am I, and so are you. . ."

Contemporary with Blake was a wonder of another order, known to most of us now through the magic of recordings and the silver screen: Johannes Chrysostomus Wolfgang Theophilus Mozart. His father called him a miracle, and by the time the boy was three was bragging about how many minuets he had learned, and in how many minutes. Daddy was an ambitious man, and dragged him and his sister Nannerl around Europe at tender ages, showing off and exposing the child prodigies to rheumatism, bad food, and sundry other dangers of 18th-century travel.

Mozart went to school in Salzburg with Haydn Minor, otherwise known as Michael, a sobersides known now practically only for his church music, but the two hit it off and Mozart was invited to dinner often at the Haydn house.

These were no genteel affairs, for Mozart was by then *der wunderkind* of Europe, composing for the Archduke Francis and quite full of himself. He had just discovered girls, and made eyes at Haydn's niece between arguments with Grandpapa Haydn over the nature of music. Mozart, as anyone who's seen *Amadeus* knows, was a genius bad boy who couldn't keep his mouth shut. He said what he thought, for he had little thought for pointless conventions. He thought life was to be lived in all its fullness. Dinner with the Haydns was just a regular part of this.

God help anyone who was not musically inclined, for with Mozart, three generations of Haydns, and whoever else might happen along, dinner often became a heated row over a passage of somebody's new composition, with much scurrying back and forth to the keyboard and banging on the table. The unmusical, like as not, would find themselves relegated to the proverbial fire escape in the midst of such passion. Instant compositions and collaborations were born of it, for Herr Mozart was an instinctive composer. In short, he heard the music of heaven in his head and brought it into denser reality.

This was his great tie with friend Haydn: his deep religious feeling, whatever you may think of Mozart's peculiarities and profanities. His masses and oratorios are the most sublime, balanced, and direct translation of heaven's music ever to come from the mind of God to man. And Mozart and Michael understood things in the same way, admired and copied from each other's works. Whatever the naughty boy might do was forgiven because of his great gift.

There are some people who think now that Mozart was subject to Tourette's syndrome—which causes the afflicted to utter profanities without provocation in the most inappropriate circumstances, but this is all bosh, a part of our modern "twinkie defense" apologies; Mozart saw the true reality, heard it in his head every day, and was impatient with the stuffed shirts of the European courts who thought themselves so enlightened and refined. In speaking aloud what they truly thought, he was poking pins in the puffed-up pigs' bladders of their egos. He was willing to make himself a fool to teach them about reality.

There is in all the organically weird a profound zest for life, and Mozart was no different. He flirted outrageously in his youth and was a favourite of many society ladies, for whom he composed beautiful arias.

In romance and family life, he proved unlucky. Thrown over by one sister—Aloysia Weber—he married the younger—Constanza—and proceeded to have several children, only two of whom lived past infancy.

How this affected him may be heard in minor-key works of the 1780s and '90s, which even to an untrained ear are troubled and chaotic compared to the light, popular pieces composed earlier.

Mozart was likely a manic-depressive, an affliction which often accompanies great gifts and is signal of the difficulties of trying to cope with living in one world while constantly experiencing another. Mozart's sister-in-law wrote that he was "even in his best periods very thoughtful, looking at one with a sharp expression. . .he seemed to be thinking deeply about something entirely different. . .his hands and feet were always in motion, he was forever playing with something, for instance, his hat, pockets, watch-chain, tables, chairs—as if he were playing the piano. . ." He was, in her words, passionately attached to the latest fads, whatever they were, perhaps to escape the too-keen reality that he knew.

By the mid-1780s, his light works were losing popularity—he was not satisfied with their frivolity in any case; he was fabulously in debt; and already caught in a cycle of manic depression, further into which the death of his father would plunge him. Several of his works in 1788—the year after his father's death—show many uncharacteristic erasures, which would indicate a violent inner turmoil. He relied heavily on his wife Constanza, some said almost desperately so, and certainly she escaped often enough to Baden to take the cure. Mozart wrote to her from Dresden, *". . .now I suppose I have written the silliest things possible (at least as far as the great world is concerned)—but for us, who love each other so dearly, it is certainly not silly—today is the 6th day I have been away from you, and by God! it seems like a year. . ."*

He depended too, on other old friends, and the Haydns did not disappoint him. In 1790, he and Joseph Haydn played together in

London. Mozart in his way saw beyond the veil, and when they parted he wept and said to his old friend, "We are probably saying our last adieus in his life." And indeed, they never met again. Though Wolfgang was only thirty-four, and Haydn Major fifty-eight, it was Mozart who died, less than a year later, all passions spent in the glorious outpouring of thirty-two years' work, burnt out as if with a comet's zeal, most brilliantly illuminated at the last.

For those modern fans of the film *Amadeus*, it is not true that Antonio Salieri killed Mozart, nor that they necessarily hated one another. The last known letter of Mozart's tells Constanza of his taking Salieri and his mistress to a performance of *The Magic Flute*, and of their response: "They both said it was a grand opera. . .they have never seen a more beautiful or pleasant production." Nor was Mozart buried in a pauper's grave. The skull long reputed to be his, lodged for many years in the musicology museum in Salzburg, was recently matched to the "best likeness" (according to his wife) of him, with the aid of modern scientific wizardry, and fitted perfectly.

Mozart's perfect hearing and translation has proofs in abundance: his music has been proved to be the favourite of unborn babies; it has soothed the insane and autistic; and most recently been shown to improve the mathematics scores of students listening to it. It sets all in alignment with the heavens, which is the true and secret purpose of the organically weird. If Mozart laughed a little too loudly, or told people what they were, we may grant him grace for the magnificent gift he gave us all.

Our next Odd Fellow is Carl Gustav Jung, who was born in 1875. Some of you may think him a "no points for guessing" individual, considering his monumental impact on our modern psychoanalytical thought process and how radical his ideas seemed at the time of their birth; but he, like Christ and Shakespeare, did not necessarily set out to be immortally famous.

But he did have a sense of moment of his own life; his enemies said to a fanatical degree. In his autobiography he went so far as to view his life as a myth, with the consequential omission of some instances—"facts" to everyone else—and magnification of others. He was, in his own mind, the Faustus of his culture.

There was much to substantiate this belief. There was the family story that his grandfather, also named Carl Gustav, was the illegitimate son of Goethe, which was never sufficiently proven nor disproven, though a relative of his who talked with the dead claimed to be the mother of this person. Jung's father was a hypochondriac minister—and a failed one at that—much given to depression. His mother was a minister's daughter, who spoke to ghosts, channeled messages from the otherworld, and otherwise unnerved poor Carl, who was susceptible enough without his mother's help. He called her a witch and was never able to overestimate her influence on him, even when she had passed into the Great Beyond. Then, she would visit him in his office, as if in dreams were not bad enough.

In his early youth, Jung wanted to be an archacologist, rummaging around in people's material rather than mental garbage, as he later did as a psychotherapist. In school everybody hated him, teachers and students alike, which may have had something to do with his nasty temper and awful pranks. Nevertheless, he viewed himself as an odd-boy-out, and to avoid the situation manifested a long episode of fainting fits, brought on ostensibly by being hit in the head by one of his fellow scholars. He could not go to school or open a book without passing out. It was his great pride that he managed to overcome this by dint of sheer will.

It's been said that old souls gravitate toward familiar occupations, either as professions or avocations, and archaeology certainly would have been comfortable. Imagine, digging up old stuff you used to know! But Carl had a pre-adolescent vision of himself as one of God's Elect, special, set apart, and hence a sense of a higher purpose.

He had flashes of old memory. Once when being told off by the father of a friend, he saw himself, in detached organically weird fashion, as being two people: one, a petulant schoolboy being reprimanded; and the other a strong, powerful old 18th-century man, far superior to the man castigating him. Jung had an uncanny, "unexplainable" familiarity with that period, its mind-set, and the detritus of its culture. He later stressed that this dissociation was not pathological; he called it normal, which psychologists then and since have found very hard to swallow.

He felt adrift in the everyday world, at odds with it, and felt he belonged to the centuries rather to the Switzerland of the 1880s and '90s. He sought solace in "God's world"; in the rocks and trees, mountains, animals. According to his own admission in his autobiography, his childhood was full of spirits and ghosts, elves and faeries. This consciousness he shared with his mother, and the thrill of it was drug-like, as anyone who has experienced it can vouch.

He questioned the nature of the universe. What was the force that compelled him to think the thoughts he did? Where did his perspicacious dreams come from?

All this led him to the breakthrough we associate with him; the realization of the "collective unconscious," or what is known today in New Age circles as the oversoul, entity, or group consciousness. That it had long been a tenet of Eastern and mystical Christian religion does not denigrate the profound impact of its advent upon our Western, material-based culture. For Jung, and seekers since him, it was a revelation. For followers of Jung's esteemed teacher, Freud, it was heresy. For the mass of humanity, it was incomprehensible humbug. What was "anima/animus" anyway? And how could we all be the embodiment of myth? In short, Jung turned the world on its ear.

The genesis of Jung's revelation lay in reading the report of a spiritualist physician, Justinus Kerner, who had discovered a medium when called upon to treat a schizophrenic. Jung devoured the work of this late-18th-century-born practitioner (who, in addition to his work using hypnosis, had also discovered botulism). Jung, on fire with the possibilities represented by Kerner's book, was delighted to discover a similar case within his own family.

A cousin of his, Helene, was a medium from his mother's side of the family. Her immediate family might be classified kindly as schizophrenics; broadly as nuts. All manner of psychic phenomena was known in their household. Helene herself was unremarkable until the age of fifteen. Her father had died and her stepmother—in true mythic Cinderella fashion—treated her badly.

She began her career using a wine glass—a primitive form of Ouija board—and soon progressed to full-trance channeling. In this state, she said that if the visible world appears to be so sharply divided from the beyond, it is only because of man's defective sense organs. In reality, transition is gradual. Hence some human beings, endowed with perfect senses, can see events invisible to the rest of mankind. Jung called his cousin's seances "the great experience which superseded my whole philosophy," and he used the case for his doctoral thesis. It did not go over well with his professor, and the two had a personal and professional break, a pattern which was to characterize Jung's life.

For, despite his philosophy, Jung was not capable of overcoming his hero-worship of anyone with whom he was connected, from his wife Emma to Sigmund Freud. He expected perfection of those he admired; and consistently, when the adored ones proved to be human after all, he castigated them savagely, dismissing them as idiots and himself as enchanted, deluded.

This struggle his detractors saw as mere manifestation of his arrogance, but it was in fact Jung's very own personal hero-journey, discriminating between the usable and the non-usable, until he came to a farther shore where he could see clearly where he had been and the dangers that were inherent in the journey. This shadow-side of his personality he called his anima. It was his word for the duality—the non-male/non-femaleness of all of us. It was his truth that we are neither male nor female, that all exists in spirit, that it is only by confronting our "dark side" and understanding it that we are to be truly made free.

He perceived the "unconscious" cosmos as orderly, though by mundane standards it may not appear so; hence the importance of analyzing dreams. It was to him a treasure trove, filled with a bounty of experiences and beings beyond ordinary fathoming, which defied clear and concise description or categorization. The purpose of its recognition was the integration of being.

In his own life, Jung could not get beyond the bounds of recognition and into practice; he never integrated all the parts of his being in a sufficient manner. He was often times crusty or downright cruel. Yet he sought perfection and found a glimpse of it in that other world, if he could not grasp it.

As Socrates was crusty and cantankerous, as Blake was impatient, as Mozart was obscene, so does every old weird soul have its Achilles Heel, its imperfection to struggle against. It is the spur toward perfection. Realization does not imply perfection, in the Buddha, in Christ, or in any guru. While mortal, we are all subject to the refraction this plane causes upon our light. The answer to judgments against this lies in looking to the stars.

And that is exactly what our last weird friend did.

Albert Einstein was born into a progressive German Jewish family, the child of free thinkers who allowed their offspring to behave differently than other children. At times they may have felt they had no choice, for little Albert was peculiar from the start.

His sister tells the story that at her birth he asked where her wheels were, as he had been promised a little sister to play with. This story is cute, the "misunderstanding" of a little child, until we look at the underlying thought processes. Then the world begins to shimmer a little, and it makes you wonder if Mama Einstein thought her child had come from Mars.

Albert later admitted to being fascinated with the way things rhymed and would spend hours in early childhood (up to the magical age of seven) softly repeating his own words. (This from a child they thought retarded because he did not talk until the age of three!

Perhaps he had nothing to say until then.) With regard to his sister and her wheels, we may think that he expected her to be like one of those little toy dogs with the string attached, until we look at the German of his question: *Raedchen/Raedle* is the German for wheel, while *Maedchen/Maedele* is the German for little girl. What dear little Albert was doing was making a very deep pun, something which he continued to enjoy all his life. This query on the part of their "retarded" child ought to have rocked the Einsteins back on their heels a bit, for it shows a very finely tuned mind, subtle and far-ranging in its thought.

When a child, Einstein asked all the questions that any organically weird child asks; and as an adult he kept asking them, which is how we all ended up being blessed with his theories of relativity and hence quantum physics. (Aren't you glad?) Einstein himself said of this, "I was brought to the formulation of the relativity theory in good part because I kept asking myself questions concerning space and time that only children wonder about." He was the eternal child.

This revelation of Einstein's has the potential to set our view of the retarded, schizophrenics, and children with so-called learning disorders on its ear. Maybe, just maybe, these people are not "idiots," but more idiot-savants, as they used to be called, like Raymond in *Rainman*. Perhaps they have a way of seeing that is closer to the true reality than our accepted mundane world view will allow for. All children and "special category" people understand Einstein's theory of relativity intuitively, for they live it every day: time and space are not separate things, but one continuum; energy becomes matter when its velocity slows down below a certain frequency; there is not merely one possibility for reality, but many.

Einstein was religious early on and was sent to a Catholic school for the educational value, where he learned religious precepts other than his native Judaism, but he kept the practices of Judaism for a long time, only later abandoning it for the non-specific religion of higher science. This "blasphemy" I would counter with Einstein's own words, that he sold himself body and soul to Science—the flight from the "I" and "we" to the "IT." For his mind and soul could no longer bear the notion of separation from all that is.

He asked himself whether God could have created a world other than this one. He questioned his reality, whether it was the only, or "true" one, and decided that it could not be, for there was much in the universe that we are incapable of physically perceiving but are capable of intuiting, or perceiving on rational faith. (Particle physics again!) He perceived, as do all old souls, the order in the seeming chaos of our accepted universe. As he said, God does not play dice.

He saw the limitations of his mind in relation to the vastness of universal reality, articulating the wonder he perceived thus:

> *The most beautiful and deepest experience a man can have is the sense of the mysterious. It is the underlying principle of religion as well as of all serious endeavour in art and in science. . .The sense that behind anything that can be experienced there is something that our mind cannot grasp and whose beauty and sublimity reaches us only indirectly and as feeble reflexion, this is religiousness. In this sense I am religious. To me is suffices to wonder at these secrets and to attempt humbly to grasp with my mind a mere image of the lofty structure of all that there is.*

This intuition was the basis for his declaration that science is metaphysics. This is not based on a view of mediaeval alchemy, but of his contemporary scientific community and his own thought processes. He argued long against the logical empiricists, who insisted that reality could be understood only by use of the scientific method, for their view left no room for the "impossible" or the intuitive, which he saw as the basis of understanding.

This is what he meant when he said that imagination is more important than knowledge. What we "know"—the "facts"—change according to whatever paradigm is current. When new "knowledge" is brought to light, you have to shift your world view entirely, or become a crank, the Flat Earth Society being a case in point.

But, if you are willing to conceive that anything is possible, then new knowledge merely adds to the purse of your perceptions and the shift is small. This is Einsteinian simplicity: the universe is harmonious in its own right; its diversity means that no one scientific theory, except recognition of that essential harmony, will encompass it all.

He disliked disharmony. A fine violinist and pianist, he reviled Beethoven's very dramatic orchestral works and preferred Bach instead, for his majesty—and he felt closest to Mozart, whose symmetry, fundamental simplicity, rational "inner perfection," went beyond the merely personal to the universal.

This love says a good deal about Mozart, but more about the place internally Einstein found himself. In modern parlance, he was seeking oneness with all that is and, in so doing, chose to perceive the harmony rather than the chaos of the universe. He lived as a child, with all a child's wonder and playfulness, and with his elucidations brought us all back home again. He would doubtless have agreed with Wordsworth that

> *Our birth is but a sleep and a forgetting*
> *The soul that rises with us, our life's Star*
> *Hath had elsewhere its setting, and cometh from afar*
> *Not in complete forgetfulness, nor in utter nakedness*
> *But trailing clouds of glory do we come*
> *From God who is our home.*

He was not the first person to think such thoughts—nor will he be the last—but he brought them into material reality for us in a way that the "logical" minds of the scientific community (our perceived saviours in his time) could accept, as one fluent in a language slows down and simplifies his speech for the struggling foreigner endeavouring to follow. He opened up for us a whole new realm of enquiry concerning reality, brought us back to ancient philosophies, full circle.

It is this journey—the great inner voyage—upon which we have all embarked. And it is the example of those that have gone "before" us that hearten us and keep us going. They are alive forever, one with us in our travels toward that farther shore, beyond which is the Sea of Infinite Bliss, Valhalla, Heaven, where all the angels greet us with open arms and emanations of Love. And the wordless greeting is *Welcome home, beloved. Your journey is done. Come dwell now in the Light.*

Chapter Thirteen

ॐ

"And Now for Something Completely Different"; or, This Just In

Since beginning the writing of this book, events have occurred which have vindicated the visions that I and others have had concerning the earth changes discussed by my guides in the last chapter. This is something of a personal validation for me, as I have spent the last nine months being thought of as a lunatic, or at least a Chicken Little, by people back in San Francisco. I have known about these changes since September of 1992, when my guides said, "There will be changes, earth changes. But the greatest change will be in the hearts of the people." What sort of changes have we experienced? Here are a few:

* There have been the floods in the American Midwest, the "inland sea" we foresaw. To judge by our winter snow, we'll likely have such floods again this year.

* There have been riots and fires in San Francisco, Los Angeles, Phoenix, and other western cities.

* Oregon, California, Brazil, and Japan have experienced earthquakes and volcanic eruptions. In short, the entire Pacific Ring of Fire is active. Just a few days before this writing, Los Angeles experienced a 6.6 earthquake which many people described as "different from anything they've ever felt before"—this from natives of the state. My friend Wendy said the same thing, and I lit on

it instantly, having only heard such reports over the television. What did she mean?

It was a rolling, she said, like standing on the deck of a ship, different too from the Simi Valley quake of 1971, which we both experienced. She said to me of the recent quake, with its aftermath of large aftershocks, broken gas mains, broken water mains, rising death toll as hospitals are evacuated, multitudes of homeless people, and current threat of dangerous mudslides and liquefaction, "I think this is the one we were expecting."

The words sent a chill through me. I know she is right. Everything is as we saw it. *Everything.* We have been granted a little time as far as the time-scale was concerned, but everything is occurring. And my thought was, "thank God I am in Virginia." It has quelled any lingering desire I had for returning to San Francisco. I have no wish to see it happen there next. I trust that Kevin has common sense about the children, and that it is not their Path to die so young.

* In the East we have had unusually cold weather this winter, with record-breaking sub-zero temperatures, which is not at all typical of Virginia. The weather is described as "arctic." As one man put it, "Global warming is a lie." We are at the advent of another mini-Ice Age, as happened in the Renaissance. The floods which will come from the melting of the heavy snowfall in the Midwest will be something to see. "An inland sea." Who can help but sit back and think, "My God, it's really happening!" Who can help but to wish to be wrong in this instance of Sight? The potential for suffering is great, and distressing. Now, I shall wait and watch to see what occurs in Europe and elsewhere, as per what we have seen.

I have heard many dates for "natural disasters," and seen a few come and go, including a hurricane here in Virginia which had the potential to devastate the lower Tidewater (Virginia Beach, as had been long predicted by Edgar Cayce and others). For whatever reason, we were spared here, for which we ought to be grateful. But many people were also angry and disappointed that the wickedness they perceived in the world (mostly technological) was not wiped out in one fell swoop.

I have learned that the changes are more insidious than the worst-case scenario represents. When we look back on the 1990s in fifty or a hundred years from now, we will surely say, as people have of the inhabitants of Crete or Pompeii, "How did they live through all that?" But while you're living it, "all that" seems mighty slow, like the drip of water upon a rock. Someday, that drip is going to cleave the rock in two, and we will look at it and remark on how suddenly it happened, without really seeing the constant drip-drip that preceded it, patiently, ever so slowly. Is it fast-occurring, or slow? That only depends on where you're standing.

I and others had been given the worst-case scenario—so as to be prepared for it. However, we were not asked to live in perpetual fear or quit our jobs, or sell our possessions; merely to be prepared for the changes. I was one to make such "drastic" changes. I know others here on this coast who have done likewise, "inexplicably" to those around them. "The greatest change will be in the hearts of the people." If we don't have a manifest reason to change, why else would we, being lazy human beings, disliking change?

Cathleen has been saying all along, as encouragement to me in my times of trouble, that I am the scout for our little group, the forerunner, the tester of the waters, the Pathfinder, the Wayfarer. I found it irksome because deep in my heart I knew it was true and didn't want to face it. Now, I *know* it to be true. And accept it. I have crossed the River Styx (the Rubicon is child's play), and I know how to help others find their own way through the personally uncharted systems of internal space, which is of course the real source of all that happens "to" us and Mother Earth. By the time really noticeable changes are manifest, I will be established enough to provide a haven for those who need or desire it.

With this acceptance of my path as a haven for those in need, I am reminded of Angharad, the (unofficial) Welsh saint whose name I was prompted to give to my daughter as a middle name. There are no accidents. That grace was as much for me as for my Ceridwen:

> *For many was her concern*
> *At nightfall, she rejoiced with many too*
> *Sensing the pain, joining the feast*
> *In the ocean of her heart was cherishing.*
> *To her doors the troubled came*
> *The weary knew the way to her court*
> *Angharad wore a scarlet gown*
> *Down to her feet; it was made of good works.*

Such I wished for my little girl, my born earth-mother Ceridwen. All the daughters of time called forth that name for her. Irene says of this: *Let her be as her mother, her grandmother, her great-grandmother, great-great-grandmother, and great-great-great-*

grandmother, who was born in a covered wagon. Let her have fortitude. Let her life be of strength. And courage. And service. Let her have an example in her mother. It was to be such an example, for her and others, that I—Kelly—was born into this time-frame. It was to be such a consoler that I have endured all the trials of my life, persecution, and sorrow. How could I have compassion if I did not experience all that myself? In the manifestation of the fulfillment of my beingness, my purpose, I bless all who have helped me get here, their kindly or unkindly actions. I am one step closer because of you. I thank you all.

In the meantime, I have the rest of this life to get through, and will endure all the physical changes this time-frame has to offer. I am taking life as it comes, making general plans with latitude and letting life fill in the rest or change the scenario as it sees fit. I have relinquished the notion of control. I do have preferences, based on past experience, and I can say that as far as future living is concerned, I vacillate between the idea of living without electricity or modern amenities of any kind, and enjoying creature comforts by having a solar-, wind-, or water-powered generator, thus facilitating electricity and all the goodies that go with it.

I have not set my mind and being immovably in either track. I am taking the teaching of Tibetan Buddhism to heart; that of the Middle Path. When someone approaches me with tales of visions of coming gloom and doom, I accept it. When someone comes to me with a heart full of love and visions of a bright shiny future, I accept it. I prefer the latter. I prefer to live in hope, for I am an idealist, but I realize that perfection does not exist here. We just have to take events as they come and focus on the good in them.

Being a late-level Old soul is like being an old anything: you look forward with relish to the comfort of your easy chair, your porch rocker, your cedar-stuffed round bed (if a dog) before the fire. Your idea of a good time is staring into space or sleeping. Then there are other times you are full of vim and vigour and want to go romping about. I can't say what my energy level will be next time, in the "vacation lifetime," the last hurrah. Icelanders are famous for "working five jobs each." In view of all I have yet to do in this life, that sounds exhausting, and I dearly hope things have loosened up a bit by the time I get there, and such hard work is not a financial necessity. Lazy old me.

Iceland may seem an unlikely and forbidding place to spend your holiday. Why not Fiji, eating breadfruit? Why a cold unknown corner of the world where they eat whale blubber and the winters are six months long?

Because I have only happy memories of the place from former times. (Bronid Patterson was a fisherman there in the 12th century; and Helgi Trondurson was a sailor in the 11th.) I want to be there precisely because "nothing" ever happens there. Iceland is an old-soul place. You never hear about it being involved in wars in the Middle East. You hardly ever hear about it at all, except once in a while when the NATO powers meet in Reykjavik on their way from somewhere else. My kind of place.

Also, Iceland is one of the places I keep returning to now and again to see how things are doing, changing. Living in the same place in a different location and time frame with different physical, political, and social structures gives one perspective, a more fully rounded picture. It has been so lately (since the last Shift) with Ireland, Scotland, and England also. With the rest of the places I have been—the Orient, the Middle East, the Mediterranean, mainland Europe—I have followed the general trend of mankind's migrations, been a part of the general scene. But my special places are so because they are at once apt to and resistent to change. I can go to Reykjavik, for instance, and experience the cutting edge of European trends, then travel a little and live life as it was millennia ago. Too much of our world has become homogeneous, plastic, for that to be true everywhere. Besides, the power at the point of the Atlantic ridge— the place of continental drift—is so strong that it tunes everything in. Lifetimes spent there are always highly charged. It would be the same if I lived in the Andes or the Himalayas, but I'm not likely to do that in the current political and social climes of those places, so Iceland it is.

The events of that life are painted in broad strokes, the exact details to be filled in as they will, according to the choice of those with whom I interact. Let us see what the future holds, how it is read. Let us look at my Icelander at thirty-five:

Helgi Thorgusson: Born September 17, 2044.
Parents: Sonja Ragnarsdottir & Thorgus Magnusson.
Siblings: brothers Ranid, Thorgus, Laedl, and Erdl. All older.
Children: son Laedl Helgisson, born 2071. The child's mother, Thula Bronidsdottir, was born 2041. Never married. The boy and his mother live now in Canada.
Physical appearance and Personality: Tall, medium build, dark brown hair, blue eyes, fair complexion. Rather weak eyesight due to

two bouts of snow blindness. He will eventually go blind in this lifetime. Left-handed. A peaceful soul, given to visions, about which he says very little. Projected age of death is mid-to-late 70s, of heart failure.

7th Level Old Warrior;
a Stoic in the Observation mode
in the Emotional part of the Intellectual centre.
No Chief Feature.
History and Hobbies:
The son of a farmer, he now farms land which has been in communal ownership in his family for 700 years. He lives thirty-seven miles NNW of Reykjavik. An amateur naturalist, he has trekked the whole of Iceland twice, sailed the Arctic Sea in a traditional Inuit boat, and mapped the migratory patterns of Icelandic birds from Norway to Greenland. He speaks Icelandic, Norwegian, Danish, English and two Inuit dialects. By profession he is by turns farmer, fisherman, musician (he plays the flute), poet, and artist. He makes woodcarvings based on the old sagas for the tourist trade and watercolours of Iceland and Greenland's flora and fauna. A scholar of the old sagas, he has gained a small measure of local fame for his lively retelling of Iceland's past. His neighbours say he has The Sight. "Almost as if he had been there," they say, at which this laconic man merely smiles. If you travel to his house, you will find simplicity of furnishings and life-style and a hearty Icelandic welcome, complete with home-made spirits. He is an easy-going host, a man of no particular ambition. He was asked to be the justice of the peace of his local village, but he refused, taking on instead the delivery of the mail. Next year he hopes to finish his handmade boat and sail to Greenland to observe the bird population there.

So much for doing nothing! Whew! But none of it is strenuous, and it all fits seamlessly together. There he is, Helgi, my Viking nerd, living a quiet, "boring" life, in which he does precisely what he pleases, without fuss. Such is the "vacation." Do I mind that the winters are six months long, full of darkness? That there is an ever-present threat of volcanic eruptions as the Mother gives birth to Herself? That I am "isolated" from the world? Nope. Not one whit. Pass me the Mediaeval Icelandic grammar and the dried fish, and call me home. Don't look me up in the phone book because there are four Helgi Thorgussons in it and you'll never guess which one is right. Ask in the village. If you can find it. And if you've found me after all that, you're welcome in for a cup of tea. Please don't mind the turpentine, and I wouldn't drink out of that dish if I were you, it belongs to the cat.

Heaven. Sheer heaven. See you around!

The above is from the Akashic Record, the imprint of all that has occurred or will occur in the physical plane. You may wonder how it is possible to "preview" the future in such a manner, there being free choice and karma and all that. The answer is disarmingly simple, an open secret yogis and other mystics have always known and that science is just discovering: the universe is really holographic. Everything exists in all its possibilities Right Now. All the past possibilities, all the future possibilities. Every place and time it is possible to be in the physical plane (that is, the whole universe) we can be at right now, as quick as a thought. Not as a theoretical possibility, but as concrete, manifest reality. This is the basis for the current "New Age" belief in "parallel universes." If you find this too weird for acceptance, thank Einstein, for it was he who cracked the egg of three-dimensional reality for the Western world.

Since Einstein, we have arrived in science at a new paradigm which is equally as radical as the theory of relativity, which bears mention here, as an explanation for the phenomenon experienced by the organically weird as our reality. I came upon this explanation thanks, once again, to Cathleen, who rang me up one day after hearing an interview on the BBC with Michael Talbot, author of *The Holographic Universe,* to tell me about Bohm's theories of holographic reality. It was very exciting, validating. She bought the book, devoured it, loaned it to me; I was struck by it, pressed it on Kevin; we all in turn bought several copies of the book and gave it to friends. This practice, similar to our reaction to the Michael books, still continues. Quantum physics for the masses. Of course, reading the Vedas, the Upanishads, or any ancient Master's work will give you the same information because there's nothing new under the sun, but Talbot's book brings ancient Truth into our own time and presents it in a way to which people living in the 20th/21st century can relate.

So what's the big news anyway? In brief, physicist David Bohm has advanced the theory that not only are time and space a continuum, being one part of all-the-same stuff, but that we all, every thing in the universe—time, space, humans, rocks, dirt, any aspect of reality you care to mention—are part of the same stuff, are all interconnected; that the universe is in truth an enormous hologram. This truth may be self-evident to the organically weird, any child, or your average tripper on LSD, but not to the mass of humanity settled into the agreed-upon time-space consensus reality of current day New York, or Tel Aviv, or Beijing.

It is known that electrons do not occupy physical space—cannot be measured, "do not exist"—until they are observed. This is the basis of holographic reality. When we look at a hologram, the picture does not exist at certain angles, or exists as a sort of amorphous mass, though all the parts exist independent of our perception of them. It is only when we view the hologram from the "right" angle that we see the picture at all, let alone in three dimensions. It is only then that the picture "becomes" reality.

Bohm's thesis began when he found that electrons in plasma behaved not in a random manner, but in a *seemingly* random manner—that when observed closely they behaved in fact as if they knew what other electrons were doing, for they made a swirling sea of a pattern under the microscope. Consciousness amongst electrons!

This wholeness is known in quantum physics as "non-locality." Essentially, at an electron level, our perceived reality of things being separate dissolves. There is no "I" and "Thou"—or mountain, rose, tiger, or anything else, including place and time. We are the same. One.

Yet we have (at least!) two realities: one of the undifferentiated mass and one of perceived separateness. For instance, I am both Kelly, in a body (which is in itself a collective reality) I have labeled such—and non-Kelly, part of the mass of the stuff of the universe.

If we expand this notion of me and not-me to its fullest potential—to "me, squared" as Cathleen recently put it—we ourselves encompass the whole of possible reality. Literally *encompass* it. "The kingdom of heaven is within," as Jesus said in the Gospel of St. Thomas, to name but one Master who tried to get this basic reality across to us slow-moving masses of universal stuff here on the physical plane. In the Sufi tradition, to give another example, there is the belief that the afterlife realm is the generative matrix ("cosmic soup") that gives birth to the entire physical universe.

Thought creates. Whatever attention we put to something, whether positive ("this is what I desire to be manifest in my reality") or negative ("I don't believe in that; that can't happen to me; I could never do something like that") we call into existence, draw the electrons together and slow them down into physical reality. *We make it happen.* This is what Irene and the Gang mean when they say there are no victims. It is the basis of reality behind the meditative admonition Be Here Now. Our focused attention on something creates the physical reality, so you might as well pay attention to what you are doing and thinking. As David Bohm states, "conscious-ness is always in the unlimited depth which is beyond space and time, in the subtler levels of the implicate order. Therefore, if you went deeply enough into the actual present, then maybe there's no difference between this moment and the next. . .Contact with eter-nity is in the present moment, but it is mediated by thought. It is a matter of attention." [*Holographic Universe*]. This is a major lesson of the physical plane. My guides are always saying, *You can do whatever you want, just be aware of what you are doing.*

We are the web and the weaver. We are all "God," creating the universe anew every moment in No Time that is Everywhere. Because the true reality is plastic (in its original sense), time, space, and every conceivable experience and perception are literally at our fingertips. For instance, I am at once sitting here writing this, and off in a far corner of the universe a million of our years from now being one with All That Is; I am a woman living in Virginia, and a semi-nomadic hunter at the edge of the European ice sheet two million years ago. I am, as I said to Kevin's student, everything and nothing. All experiences are mine if I agree to experience them free-flowingly. Anything is possible if we turn the locality switch of our time-and-space-bound mind to nonlocality, if we believe any-thing is possible. Any time is perceivable if we accept that it is. (Which is an answer to the question "why do old souls and crazies experience past lives and alternative forms of reality when the rest of us can't?") This is the secret of yogic tradition and New Age "magic." I can turn off blood flow to a wound and heal it instantly or finish Mahler's unfinished symphony as he intended. Think it, be there, do it. Anything is possible because nothing really "is" until we make it so. The universe is really just a vast playground for us all.

This holographic reality is basis of every psychic phenomenon experienced on this plane, from "precognition" and "past"-life recall to psychokinesis, manifestation of objects, and shamanistic shape-shifting. It is the secret of the physical plane that we guard from ourselves until we have expanded enough in consciousness for it to be an exciting realization and not a frightening one.

For it *will* be frightening to the slower-moving fragments—the podlings and Baby souls of this earth—for to the slow-moving electron, the fast-moving appears chaotic. It is only when our fre-quency of vibration increases that we get into the swing of things and begin to perceive that there is a rhythm and a pattern to the swift movement, much as it is difficult to discern the parts of a skater's programme or ballet dance without being a skater or a dancer.

To the untrained observer, all is awesome, spectacular, because the whole is merely a sum of its parts, of which we cannot conceive. But to the dancer or skater, the whole is broken down into a sum of its parts and something else which goes beyond mere technique, and which is impossible to describe succinctly. That *something* is the unifying principle, the holographic flow, and it too is awesome, magical, but in a very different way from our earlier perceptions.

As Irene and the Gang say, *We "old folks" remember our first view of the world and our wonder at it, and when we are among the initiates, it is no less wonderful, but we view it differently. It is not true that we have forgotten how difficult it was to learn. In fact, we recall better than those immersed in learning, for we are not so narrowly focused. We can see the forest for the trees, understand the art behind technique, literally embody the force behind supposedly impossible phenomena, and we call to those following us with encouragement, for we have a clear view of paradise, and it is worth the hazards of the road "there".*

Chapter Fourteen

ॐ

The Secret

The following is the Extremely Lazy version (to steal a leaf from Thaddeus Golas) of this book, and it was the experience of my editor and dear friend, Frank DeMarco, who has so admirably played his part as a catalyst for transformation in my life (take a bow, Frank). But he would say the same of me in his life, and so would Cathleen, and Wendy, and assorted other dear ones, for we all facilitate one another. This came as a sort of interactive automatic writing, what he calls talking to "The Gentlemen Upstairs." If you question its validity, please take note that on reading it several days after its transmission, I rang Frank up and asked in good old Warrior comradely friendly outrage: "How come you didn't tell me you got it!!!!" His reply was simply, "I didn't think it was any big deal"—which is an excellent illustration of the seventh step on the path to Nirvana; taking no pride in having achieved the former six. I offer it as it was given to me in February of this year, with only minor editing (as you will see) for clarification:

Saturday, February 12, 1994 1:25 a.m.
Kelly says she wishes I would just "get it." Well, I'm certainly willing. Gentlemen, what do I need to do to finally "get it"?

You will recall that when you met her you were still in the mode of always asking "how do I know this is true? How do I know I am not making this up because I want it to be true? How does she know, how do I know, that she isn't faking it on some level conscious or, more likely, semi-conscious or unconscious?" Aware that you were more than willing to believe what you wanted to be true, you were also crippling yourself by refusing to accept what in fact you knew.

You have come a long way since that, in a short time, however long or short it may appear to you. Merely remember the process by which you came to know; this has two reasons behind it, not just one. Besides the remembering what it is to remember (the process, which you are aware of, and have been in advance, as she mentioned it that first night in October [when I, Kelly, had traveled to Virginia for a Jefferson conference. My remark was typical of me: "What's the matter with you, Frank? You know all this stuff!"]) there is the fact that now you also know how you got here and know that you didn't "skip" a stage; you didn't merely decide to go from there to here and therefore decided you *were* here.

Recalling the care you have taken not to delude yourself, now remember that this is only half the process, the other half being taking care not to cripple your recall by instantly distrusting whatever comes instinctively.

Do you want to "get it"? Then, merely, trust yourself. Trust at your deepest levels. Stop distrusting what comes naturally. Stop allowing your instinct to be distrusted or overruled by your reason, or rather your reasoning. Mostly you have done the latter: reasoning is no longer allowed to overrule; all you need do now is go that final step, and not allow reasoning even to distrust.

You ask, "then how will I protect myself from becoming a fool, believing whatever I want to believe." Know, instead, that there's a reason for what you want to believe.

You know, you have seen, that:

1) People believe what they want to believe.

2) People don't do things, feel things, think things, without reasons, regardless whether they know those reasons.

3) What you believe is what is real for you—and don't attempt to sort out which came first, the chicken or the egg. You do create your own reality, everyone does, and you realize that now. Well, before you realized that, you doubted it; denied it; derided the very idea. Then things happened that changed who you are, which changed what you believed, which changed who you are, which changed what you believe. Where is the beginning of this process? Not anywhere recent, but long before you were born into

any of your lifetimes. And it is so for everyone. Believe this. Know it.

End self-distrust. Yes, I can see that. Is there a "how" to that?

There is a time and season to everything. By being ready to ask the proper question, you made yourself ready/showed that you are ready/merely demonstrated the results of the fact that you *are* ready. Circular logic for a circular process. You are free. As Kelly said long ago, "choose a reality, make it so." Now you know.

God bless her, I believe I do know. Can I now remove downstairs and receive the information I have wanted all this time?

Why not?
You expected a cautionary, "don't expect too much at one time," etc. because it seems too good to be true, and you fear disappointment. But it is as in December, 1992 [when he went to a course at The Monroe Institute which revealed to him some of his power]. You asked if you would ever get what you really wanted, and were told it was merely a matter of learning—and came to know that this was no empty promise. Now, you are told it is available to you on the cessation of internal opposition. Go, what you want is in your hand—unless you choose to refuse it.

Saturday, February 12, 1994 2:02 a.m.
Can you tell me how to use internet to get the confirmations that would help? Kelly I notice put plenty of effort into confirmations.

Of course, and this is how it should *be* done. Intuition first, logic a long way second. As you have long known and now realize (i.e. it is a little more real to you) more deeply. As you go find, we will help you retrieve validations. As we always have.

Thank you.

Saturday, February 12, 1994 10:31 a.m.
Having set out to T[he] M[onroe] I[nstitute], gotten 40 miles, and returned. I felt it was the right decision because the [snow-covered]

roads, while more than passable, were littered with accidents, at least four or five in 40 miles. And I suppose this was the right decision. Is there any particular reason for this delay?

> If nothing else, this will serve to remind you that you need not be somewhere special to be where you need be; that you need not be surrounded by specific others, or any other; that you are free internally as soon as you realize your freedom. You saw this with Kelly, now see it with TMI and indeed with everything external and internal. Freedom consists in the ability to maintain your position regardless of circumstances. It lies, in other words, in holding yourself, or rather (lest that seem too active and tense a process) in not losing yourself to circumstance. Now you are here at home for an unexpected day, after a day at work rather than home, also unexpected, and a shortened day before that, also unexpected. So what is your choice? To be thrown off the rails by every newt's wing? Or to roll relentlessly on, casually, remorselessly, serenely? This is not a choice, put thus baldly. The difficulty is in the living, or rather the difficulty is in the acceptance of the possibility of so living.

Saturday, February 12, 1994 8:06 p.m.
A long conversation with TGU earlier today, written in my journal a little after 4:30 p.m.:

I am now talking to The Gentlemen Upstairs. Let me first talk to Evangeline. [One of his guides, an "old friend," whom he had "neglected" for a while.] Have you missed me? Are you part of the group we call TGU? Are you other?

> Know, dear love, that we are always with you so far as you are concerned—that when you call in any way, we are there. It is not a matter of our being off-duty where you are concerned. The aspects of oneself/yourself that are called into play do not negate the existence of other aspects, doing other things.
>
> Yes I am one of The Gentlemen Upstairs, but you needn't therefore begin to refer to us as the Ladies and Gentlemen Upstairs!
>
> What is important is that you do listen and speak and thus open yourself up to the unfolding of what you already

are—paradoxical though this may sound. Know well, beloved friend, how far you have come, how quickly. This is because you began only from a self-inflicted (if you choose to call it that) position of inferior access. This is part of the play [sic] you had, and has proceeded according to plan.

Evangeline, who were you last? You *were* in a body?

Oh yes. 1700s in America and you knew me well, though you remember it not. And hark,—to answer Kelly's perplexity about Thomas [Jefferson] finishing "first" [before Patty] by so long a margin. It is true as has been said by more than one who woke up that lives are not lived sequentially, there being no sequence. Believe me, I remember how hard it "was" to understand such a statement, being immersed in space/time Theater. Do not undertake to make too much sense of it, lest you cover with logic that which is better seen as pure as possible. Rather than giving yourself a headache trying to make it logically sensible, just accept it and move on—your lives from your soul's point of context (if you will) is a mosa—-is a pattern fitted into the play around you, the world. Quick, we need a bit player in Phoenicia, 2000 BC. I'll do it! Okay, you're on. And how about one in 1500 AD in a monastery in mid-France. OK. Good. Now India, 500s? Sure. America, several successive lives. England. What you now call Antarctica, with which, it should be obvious, you have a *significant* attachment, built over many lifetimes.

If you can think of yourself as playing these many roles, as signing up for these many roles, in advance, and appearing on the various sound-stages as they are filmed, you will have a better analogy to your situation. You can easily think of films being filmed out of order; to think of everything happening out of time is beyond you given your constraints. Don't worry about it, it's enough to know the illusion is only that.

So you see, if Thomas' final part is in 1815 or 1915 or 2015, it has nothing to do with comparisons of another dear friend whose last part is in 1860 or 1960 or 2060. You see? When a film is being made, or what era the film portrays, says nothing about the state of a given actor's advancement. Is there a prize for filling your engagements first and being the first to go off on vacation?

Particularly as there is no first. And this is what is hard for you to realize. *At any given time,* "we" are "up here" and "you" are "down there"—regardless *where* or *who.* Do you understand? For Thomas (Matthew, whatever) [Matthew was Thomas' name in his "last" life] there are all those realities in which "The Gentlemen Upstairs" comprise, among others—you! As we do to you now. It is only in the mesh of a particular lifetime that one is ever "separated" from the other players. Among whom is oneself! Not one's *past* self, or *future* self, or *part of* one's self, but one's self. I know this is nearly impossible for you to understand but you can get it close enough, else we would not bring this forward now. And "we," we would remind you, is the plural of "I".

To return to the original question after this truly very interesting discussion?

We smile. Your uncle isn't the only stubborn one in your family.

John Cotten—John James Cotten—had a sweetheart named Annabelle when he was very young. 14 perhaps. That particular case of puppy-love came to nothing, as the world counts things, as she and her family moved on west into Ohio territory (as it became) but it served to hold the place, as it were. It was as you and Kelly coming within sight one of the other [London, 1907; Wales 1887] even if no more—it helped the other remember connection and not feel quite so isolated.

Annabelle Jenkins lived from 1749 to 1798, just nearly 50 years, a good life span for the time. She was a wife and mother and led a totally unremarkable life, becoming a frontier wife, mother and grandmother. Dying not of violence but of weariness of body and readiness of soul. This particular role was her final role.

Now—note that Annabelle was not the realized being you seem to think the "final" lifetime requires, because this was the "final" lifetime only in chronology, which machs nicht here. My "final" lifetime from my context was the one from which I realized the illusion of time and separation—which you dear friend are in the process of accomplishing, as per plan, and our congratulations to

182

you. But you see, your "final" lifetime from that point of view—the only one that makes sense from here, though it doesn't make all *that* much sense, given the illusory nature of time—your "final" lifetime may occur centuries, millennia in "time" "before" other lives. Can you sense that chronology doesn't have anything intrinsic to do with it? It's just the shooting schedule.

Kelly is firmly of the opinion that her final lifetime will be a resting lifetime in Iceland, some years hence (from our point of view). (I should put "will be" in quotes, I suppose.) Does your statement mean that it could as easily be in the 1700s?

Yes. And we question a clinging to a single scenario. Shooting schedules change, films are cancelled or postponed, directors are hired or fired, sound stages are disrupted by strikes or even earthquakes. [Helgi's life as portrayed herein is the basic script as far as general consensus of the group is concerned. As with any script, it is open to re-interpretation, total overhaul, or chucking out entirely. This is the Middle Path.]

So Helgi may not be cleaning fish for 70 years in the future?

We say only this: put not too much investment into any *one* way of seeing things, including what comes from us. Freedom lies between scripts, not within any or all of them.

Appendix I

ॐ

From Here to Eternity; or, Days of Our Lives

Since you have traveled along with me a bit on my journey and have seen the influences that have made me what I am, I thought you might like a broader view of the field than was possible to give in the text. The following list of lifetimes is subject to revision as my "gap" periods, where there are few resonances in this life, are filled in. You'll notice there's generally not much of a gap between lives; this is a common Warrior trait.

1963-
Kelly Joyce Neff

1944-1961
Richard Bunton, born in Liverpool, England, of middle-class parents. An artist, he died of an unintentional overdose of cocaine and heroin. Tall, very thin, brown hair, hazel eyes, fair complexion, medium build.

1928-1942
Markus _____, born in Prague to an oculist and his wife. An ethnically Polish Jew, he grew up in _____ Poland. Was sent to Auschwitz in 1941. Died at Birkenau in February, 1942. Brown-haired, brown-eyed, fair-skinned, of slight build.

1891-1928
Mary Clennaghan Leary. Born in Dublin, Ireland, of upper-class parents. A classical pianist and equestrienne. Married a Trinity don. Died of tuberculosis. Tall, black-haired, grey-eyed, of slender build.

1866-1889
Emily Catton. Born near Cardiff, Wales, of upper-class parents. A watercolourist. Died of tuberculosis. Medium height, blonde-haired, blue-eyed, of medium build.

1843-1865
Eleanor Simpkin Markham. Born in Judy Gap, West Virginia. Dressmaker. Married a schoolteacher. Died in a fire in Quinter, Kansas. Tall, brown-haired, brown-eyed, of medium build.

1788-1832
Robert Lescaux. Born in Cape Breton, Nova Scotia. Sailor. Press-ganged by the British in the War of 1812. Fell from the mast and drowned going round Cape Horn. Short, golden-brown hair, blue-grey eyes, medium build.

1748-1782
Martha Wayles Jefferson. Born in Charles City Co., Virginia. Plantation mistress. Played the keyboard and guitar. Died of diabetes. Short, dark-auburn hair, hazel eyes, medium complexion, slight build.

1704-1746
Thomas MacEwan. Born outside Aberdeen, Scotland. Cooper. Fought for Bonny Prince Charlie. Survived Culloden. Joined British army. Died in Ireland, by a blow to the head. Tall, black-haired, blue-eyed, medium build.

1633-1702
Lelia O'Tuohy Larkin. Born outside Ennis, County Clare, Ireland. Midwife. Ran an illegal public house. Accused of immorality and witchcraft. Died of old age. Tall, auburn hair, hazel eyes, medium complexion, stout build.

1570-1623
Margaret MacLeod. Born at Dunvegan, Isle of Skye. Sister of the Clan Chief. Married chief of Clan Donald. Accused of witchcraft and infanticide. Marriage annulled. Died in a nunnery in Ireland of a heart condition. Short, black hair, black eyes, medium complexion, slight build.

1540-1568
Phillipe de Gueilliac. Born in Paris, France. Tailor. Apprenticed to his father. Made clothing for the emerging merchant gentry. Died of tuberculosis. Short, brown hair, brown eyes, medium complexion, medium build.

1485-1533
Maurice du St. Germaine. Born in Lorraine, France. Monk, herbalist. An orphan, left as a toddler at the monastery where he spent his entire life. Grew up in the kitchen. Was taken up by the brother herbalist. Never took full orders. Died of heart failure in his garden. Medium height, ginger hair, grey eyes, fair complexion, stout build.

1435-1471
"Raji." Born in the foothills of the Tibetan Himalayas. Monk, physician. Youngest son of a farmer of Nepalese/Indian ethnicity, was taken to the monastery at fourteen because there were too many mouths to feed. Proved adept at healing, was taught medicine. Traveled much in connection with his work. Chose to enter a hermitage at thirty-three. Died of a head injury. Tall, black hair, brown eyes, medium complexion, slight build.

1397-1429
Robert_____. Cluniac monk. Son of a potter, married young, wife died. Entered monastery at the age of 23. Never took full orders. Died of exposure. Short, golden-brown hair, green eyes, fair complexion, medium build.

1325-1390
German Burgher. A merchant, with early army service. Extremely ambitious and widely intolerant, he accrued much karma due to his "when in Rome" philosophy (rather unsuccessfully trying to settle into being an old soul). Died of apoplexy. Short, ginger hair, grey eyes, florid complexion, stout build.

1278-1316
English Tinker. Born in the Cotswolds. Traveled about the country mending pots and trading horses. Died of exposure. Tall, brown hair, hazel eyes, medium complexion, thin.

1234-1275
Ancel Bronin. Cistercian monk. Born near Salisbury, England. joined the priesthood at an early age, took full orders in the Order of St. Martin Magnus. Oversaw the scriptorium. Was a member of a secret mystical society within the order. Saw the building of Salisbury Cathedral. Died of a brain embolism. Tall, dark-brown hair, grey eyes, medium, sallow complexion, medium build.

1186-1220
Merfyn Caermac. Born in Glamorganshire, Wales. Accidentally killed his brother, ran away to London, where he became involved in court intrigue as a servant to a nobleman. Hanged himself. Medium height, black hair, brown eyes, medium complexion, slender build.

1135-1184
Bronid Patterson. Fisherman. Born in Iceland. Fished, had a large family, a placid and jovial life. A resting lifetime. Drowned. Medium height, medium, brown hair, blue eyes, fair complexion, stout build.

1109-1135
Enid Ragnarsdottir. Housewife. Born in Iceland. A resting lifetime, like the last. Married, had six children, died of a fever in the winter. Medium height, light brown hair, hazel eyes, fair complexion, medium build.

1065-1107
Helgi Trondursson. Sailor. Born in Iceland. Fancied himself a poet, illuminated sagas in his idle hours. A peaceful soul. another resting life. Drowned. Tall, blond hair, green eyes, florid complexion, medium build.

968-1042
Lorcan O'Tuohig. Very minor local chieftain. Born in Wexford, Ireland. Sought peace between his people and the Vikings. Married his daughter (against her will) to the local Viking chief as an alliance. Fought at Clontarf for Brian Boru. Died of wounds. Tall, red hair, grey eyes, florid complexion, stout build.

927-964
Anama Noddid. Pictish warrior. Born near Maes Howe, Orkney (Scotland). Spent his life fighting the infiltration of Orkney by the

Scoti (Irish) and Norse (a lost cause from the beginning). Married two wives (concurrently), had 14 children, 6 of whom lived past infancy. Died of wounds and exposure. Short, black hair, black eyes, medium complexion, medium build.

842-917

Meidbh ni Cu Uladh. Daughter of a minor chieftain. Born near Blackrock, Co Dublin, Ireland. Had a brief liason with a Vikibng, for which she was shunned. Joined a group of women religious and became a seeress. Died of heart failure. Short, blonde hair, green eyes, fair complexion, slight build.

832-41

Norse boy. Frail due to a congenital heart defect, spent his short life lying abed, listening to the storyteller. Had visions, and was regarded as *wyrrd*. Died of heart failure. Small, brown hair, hazel eyes, fair complexion, slight build.

6th C. Common Era.

Katerine Ernster. Born in Bavaria. Housewife. A jovial person, married a goatherd, had 20 children, 13 of whom lived past infancy. Died of fever, late middle age, mid 50s. Tall, blonde hair, blue eyes, florid complexion, stout build.

5th C. Common Era.

Padme _____. Born in Delhi, India. Daughter of a spice merchant. Married her cousin, helped in the family business, had seven children and a fat happy life. Died of stroke in late middle age, about 60 years. short, black hair, brown eyes, medium complexion, slender build, but ran to fat in later life.

136-164 Common Era.

British man. Born near the Antonine Wall. A warrior of mixed Pictish and Celtic descent. Died of wounds. Medium height, medium brown hair, hazel eyes, florid complexion, medium build.

65-79 Common Era.

Roman girl. Born in Herculaneum. Died in the eruption of Vesuvius. Tall, golden-brown hair, brown eyes, fair complexion, slight build.

06-63 Common Era.
Juliana Antonia. Born in Rome. Cousin of Tiberius and Claudius, married a Senator, Paulinas Antonius. Had four children. Hosted a party for Caractacus, the Briton, when he was brought to Rome. Spent her time doing good works. A resting life.

Died of heart failure. Medium height, brown hair, brown eyes, medium complexion, stout build.

50-28 BCE
Roman soldier. Born in Etruria. Joined the army as a career, went to Syria and Judea. Never married. Died from a blow to the head. Short, dark brown hair, brown eyes, medium complexion, medium build.

1390s-1360s BCE
Mycenaean sailor. Fought at Troy, died there. Short, black hair, brown eyes, medium complexion, slight build.

1668-1626 BCE
Car (Cybele). Temple priestess. Born in eastern Crete. Daughter of a woodcarver who made votives for the king, she was dedicated to temple service as a child. Drowned. Tall, golden brown hair, light brown eyes, medium complexion, slender build.

Temple priestess. Phoenicia.

Assyrian man. Merchant.

Babylonian man. Labourer.

15th Dynasty. Egypt.
Physician. Surgeon. Served the royal family. Took to preparing the dead later in life. Died of heart failure in extreme old age.

Short, black hair, brown eyes, medium-to-dark complexion, slight build.

Sumerian man.

10,000 BCE Midlothian (Scotland)
Hunter's wife. This at the end of the last Ice Age. Lived at the upper edge of the European Ice Sheet. Husband was a shaman. When he died she married his brother. A hardy soul. Died of heart failure

in late middle age (about 40). Medium height, dark brown hair, brown eyes, fair-to-medium complexion, medium build.

3 M BCE
Woman. North Africa. Hunter-gatherer society, had some herbal knowledge. Fell into an underground cave, died of wounds in early middle age (about 26). Medium height, black hair, brown eyes, medium-to-dark complexion, slender build.

3 M BCE
Woman. East Africa. Hunter-gatherer society. Shaman's daughter, became a medicine woman herself. Married three times, had no living children. Died of heart failure in old age (late 60s). Short, black hair, brown eyes, medium-to-dark complexion, slender build.

Before Last Shift.
Merchant. Dealt in all manner of goods. Was an extremely jealous man, had his wife's lover killed. Died of stroke in late middle age. Tall, dark brown hair, green eyes, medium complexion, stout build.

Appendix II

The Return of the Appendix; or, Entertainment Tonight (Music, Books, and Movies for the Organically Weird)

Of films with a message, those that connect deeply with the true reality, I have the following list of favourites. You likely will find your own to add to it:

Aladdin
Amadeus
Back to the Future
Baraka
Being There
Benny and Joon
Brigadoon
Brother Sun, Sister Moon
City of Joy
Dances With Wolves
Darby O'Gill and the Little People
The Dark Crystal
Dead Again
Dead Poets Society
Defending Your Life
ET
Excalibur
Far and Away
The Field
Finnian's Rainbow
Flatliners

FoxFire
Ghost
Groundhog Day
Hair
Harold and Maud
Heart and Souls
Highlander
High Spirits
The Hobbit
Hocus Pocus
Hook
Iceman
Indiana Jones and the Last Crusade
Joseph and the Amazing Technicolor Dreamcoat
Labyrinth
Ladyhawke
The Last of the Mohicans
Legend
Little Buddha
The Man From Snowy River
Medicine Man
Oh God
On A Clear Day You Can See Forever
Orlando
The Princess Bride
Rainman
Star Trek (I)
Star Wars (trilogy)
Sunshine
Time After Time
Watership Down
Willow
The Wind in the Willows
The Wizard of Oz

Of music, I find the works and artists below especially helpful for tuning in. The range is from classical to pop and "New Age." Some of it may seem improbable as uplifting and "spiritual," but truth is where you find it, and in my book, anything that celebrates life is A-OK when I'm feeling stuck.

Scott Appel
The Bach Family (any of them)
Hildegard von Bingen
The Byrds
The Beatles
Mary Black
Carmina Burana
Clannad
Archangelo Corelli
Phil Coulter
Country Joe & the Fish
Crosby, Stills & Nash
Constance Denby
John Denver
Donovan
Enya
The Grateful Dead
Gregorian Chant (any)
George Frideric Handel
George Harrison
Joseph Haydn
Michael Haydn
Jethro Tull
Jefferson Airplane/Starship
Billy Joel
Elton John
John Lennon
Manheim Steamroller
Rick Miller
Van Morrison
Wolfgang Amadeus Mozart
R. Carlos Nikki
Johann Pachelbel
Henry Purcell
Queen
Andy M. Stewart
Sting
Ralph Vaughan-Williams
Antonio Vivaldi
Andreas Vollenweider

In reading matter, I have made no discrimination between "serious" works and "frivolous," for truth is often said in jest, and children often have the keys to doors adults can never find. Here are some of my favourites, in no particular order:

The Lazy Man's Guide to Enlightenment by Thaddeus Golas
Meditations for the New Age, edited by Carol Tonsing
Ageless Body, Timeless Mind, by Deepak Chopra, M.D.
Creating Affluence, by Deepak Chopra, M.D.
The Tao of Pooh by Benjamin Hoff
The Tao te Ching by Lao Tsu
The Teachings of the Compassionate Buddha, edited by E.A. Burtt
Ocean of Wisdom by the Dalai Lama of Tibet
Tibetan Yoga, and Secret Doctrines, edited by W.Y. Evans-Wentz
The Tibetan Book of the Dead, edited by W.Y. Evans-Wentz
The Bhagavad Gita, translated by Shri Purohit Swami
The Secret Teachings of Jesus, translated by Marvin W. Meyer
The Koran

Beowulf
The Epic of Gilgamesh
The Illiad
The Odyssey
Gawain and the Green Knight
Percival
The Song of Roland
La Morte d'Arthur by Thomas Mallory

The Third Eye by T. Lobsang Rampa
Doctor From Lhasa by T. Lobsang Rampa
The Prophet by Kalill Gibran
Be Here Now by Ram Dass
Journey of Awakening by Ram Dass
Shambala, the Sacred Path of the Warrior by Chogyam Trungpa
The Cheese and the Worms by Carlo Ginzburg

The Magic Mountain by Thomas Mann
Death in Venice by Thomas Mann
Siddhartha by Hermann Hesse
Steppenwolf by Hermann Hesse

Thus Spoke Zarathustra by Friedrich Nietzsche
Frankenstein by Mary Shelley
The Last Man by Mary Shelley
Robinson Crusoe by Robert Louis Stevenson
The Swiss Family Robinson by Robert Louis Stevenson
Gulliver's Travels by Jonathan Swift
Tristram Shandy by Laurence Sterne
Ulysses by James Joyce
Finnegan's Wake by James Joyce
John Lennon in Heaven, by Linda Keen
City of Joy, by Dominique Lapierre
Life 101, by John-Roger and Peter McWilliams
The Mists of Avalon by Marion Zimmer Bradley
Outlander by Diana Gabaldon
Dragonfly in Amber by Diana Gabaldon
Seventh Son by Orson Scott Card

The Adventures of Winnie the Pooh by A.A. Milne
The World of Christopher Robin by A.A. Milne
The Secret Garden by Frances H. Burnett
The Little Princess by Frances H. Burnett
The Wizard of Oz by Frank L. Baum
Alice in Wonderland by Lewis Carroll
Through the Looking Glass by Lewis Carroll
The Velveteen Rabbit by Marjorie Williams
Charlotte's Web by E.B. White
The Earthsea Trilogy by Ursula K. LeGuin
The Chronicles of Narnia by C.S. Lewis
The Lord of the Rings Trilogy by J.R.R. Tolkien

The Secret Life of Plants by Peter Tompkins and Christopher Bird
Subtle Energy by John Davidson
The Holographic Universe by Michael Talbot
Messages From Michael by Chelsea Quinn Yarbro
More Messages from Michael Chelsea Quinn Yarbro

John Keats
Henry David Thoreau
Percy Bysse Shelley
William Butler Yeats
William Wordsworth
Dylan Thomas

Samuel Taylor Coleridge
Alfred, Lord Tennison
Lord Byron
Walt Whitman
D.H. Lawrence
John Donne

About the Author

Kelly Joyce Neff was born in Los Angeles, California, in 1963. She received her degree in Celtic Studies from San Francisco State University in 1986 after doing fieldwork in descriptive linguistics in Ireland. She speaks Irish, Scots, Welsh and Breton, and "enough French and German to get me to the bathrooms and to the public houses." She has worked as dancer, singer and actress, and is a practicing herbalist and traditional midwife. Currently she lives in Williamsburg, Virginia, where she works as researcher and character interpreter for Colonial Williamsburg. In her spare time she writes and does channeling and psychic healing. She is the author of an as-yet-unpublished biography of Martha Jefferson.

She was married to Kevin Quattrin (author of *Living in a Psychic's World*). They have three children: Rudraigh Callaghan, Cian Amergin, and Ceridwen Angharad.

Books of Related Interest

Living In a Psychic's World: A True-Life Experience
Kevin Quattrin

In a very real sense, psychics and non-psychics live in different worlds. This book is Kevin Quattrin's reflections on his experience of marriage to Kelly Joyce Neff (author of *Everyday Life in Two Worlds*), a talented psychic whose abilities he recognized, and whose world he could share—to a degree. Told with humor and honesty, *Living in a Psychic's World* will be of great value to others who find themselves sharing the same household while living in different worlds. *ISBN 1-878901-94-X, $9.95*

* * * * * *

Born With a Veil
Maya Perez with Terry A. Latterman

Author and psychic investigator Jess Stearn (*Edgar Cayce, The Sleeping Prophet*) has called Maya Perez "the greatest psychic of them all." Here for the first time she tells the full story of her life as a spiritual mystic. *ISBN 1-878901-04-4, $9.95*

Mind Trek: Exploring Consciousness, Time, and Space Through Remote Viewing
Joseph McMoneagle

Not least among the underrated powers of the human mind is the ability to "see" in the mind's eye things that are remote in time and/or space. This innate ability, seemingly well-developed at birth in some, can be learned. In *Mind Trek*, Joseph McMoneagle, a remote viewer for more than 20 years, tells how he developed his abilities and gives the reader guidelines on how to follow in his footsteps. *ISBN 1-878901-72-9, $10.95*

Past Lives, Future Growth
Armand Marcotte and Ann Druffel

Mr. Marcotte, a professional clairvoyant consultant, is often used by the police to solve cases involving murder, missing persons, etc. His other clients' problems range widely: abortion, incest,

homosexuality, suicide, and problems of marriage and divorce. Working with the help of his spirit guides, he helps people understand the roots of their problems, so that they can begin to work them out. Interestingly, Marcotte very frequently finds that people's present problems have their roots in previous lifetimes.
ISBN 1-878901-79-6, $8.95

Red Snake
George McMullen

George McMullen, a psychic who became famous for his work in "psychic archeology," here relates the life of a Native American who lived among the Iroquois in the days before the coming of the white Europeans—as told psychically by Red Snake himself. This fascinating story provides an unequaled glimpse of everyday life in a vanished culture. *ISBN 1-878901-58-3, $9.95*

Soulmaker: True Stories from the Far Side of the Psyche
Michael Grosso
Foreword by Whitley Strieber

Have we moderns lost our souls? The author of this brilliant book says yes—and demonstrates it, using fascinating, down-to-earth examples from his own life and the lives of those around him. Grosso invites the reader to think with him—about drugs and dreams, astral sex and symbols, time and ghosts and the meaning of the strange lives we all lead. *ISBN 1-878901-21-4, $9.95*

Traveling With Power: The Exploration and Development of Perception
Ken Eagle Feather

A ground-breaking book on the nature of consciousness and the varieties of perception. From instructions on out-of-body travel to conversations with Pleiadeans, the author takes us on a journey which involves shamanism, earth changes, the mystical experience, leading-edge technologies, the practical use of dreaming, blending science and mysticism in a manner which helps clarify both, and ultimately the elusive nature of life on the planet earth.
ISBN 1-878901-28-1, $10.95

Hampton Roads publishes a variety of books on metaphysical,
spiritual, health-related, and general interest subjects.
Would you like to be notified as we publish new books in your area of
interest? If you would like a copy of our latest catalog, just call
toll-free, (800) 766-8009, or send your name and address to:

Hampton Roads Publishing Company, Inc.
891 Norfolk Square
Norfolk, VA 23502